AUDIO ACCESS INCLUDED

FINGERSTYLE GUITAR TUNINGS

DADGAD & BEYOND

Progressive Techniques and Concepts for the Modern Guitarist

BY DANNY HEINES

T0071462

PLAYBACK+
Speed • Pitch • Balance • Loop

To access audio visit:
www.halleonard.com/mylibrary

Enter Code
8361-5046-0788-8562

ISBN 978-1-4950-8939-8

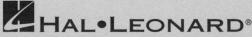

HAL•LEONARD®

7777 W. BLUEMOUND RD. P.O. BOX 13819 MILWAUKEE, WI 53213

In Australia Contact:
Hal Leonard Australia Pty. Ltd.
4 Lentara Court
Cheltenham, Victoria, 3192 Australia
Email: ausadmin@halleonard.com.au

Visit Hal Leonard Online at
www.halleonard.com

TABLE OF CONTENTS

PREFACE

While there are many books on the market on the subject of alternate tunings, I have yet to find a universal method for mapping a new tuning and navigating its harmony. Without a logical method of navigation, we can only follow our ear, often relying heavily upon trial and error. While this approach can lead to interesting discoveries, it generally gives us only a limited set of options with which to explore a tuning. The ability to see the harmonic architecture of a tuning, along with using your ears, is the key to unlocking its potential.

Coming to the world of alternate tunings many years ago as a jazz guitarist well versed in theory, I was able to easily map out the notes of a key or keys that reflected the tonality of a new tuning. This led to establishing and expanding a vocabulary of chords and scales with which to improvise and compose in a solo guitar context. This method, which has now evolved over many years, is clearly demonstrated in this book using a hands-on approach. We'll also be covering many other aspects of playing in modern modal tunings, including right-hand technique, slapping, tapping, and much more.

Whether you're new to alternate tunings or have been using them for years and just want to deepen your understanding, I believe you'll find this book extremely useful. As the book develops, we'll be covering some fairly advanced concepts, but I have provided a step-by-step approach that will allow even those who are new to alternate tunings or music theory to learn and integrate the material.

If you're an experienced player and have a thorough understanding of diatonic and pentatonic harmony, you may find that you can go very quickly through, or skip altogether, Section One: "Theory Essentials."

Feel free to work at a pace that is right for you. If you find something confusing, make sure you have read and fully understand the preceding sections. Most of the chapters proceed with the assumption that all previous chapters are fully understood. If you run across a musical term with which you're unfamiliar, use the Glossary in the Reference Section to learn its meaning before going on.

Lastly, keep in mind that music theory should never replace using your ears or intuition in a creative way. Theory should function rather like a roadmap. You look at it before you begin a journey, or when you get lost. If you kept your eyes glued to the map, you'd miss the scenery and probably drive into a tree. If you already know the way, you don't even need to look at the map. In other words, the better your understanding of theory, the less you have to think about it. Ultimately, let your ears and artistic sense be the final judge and be sure to renew your artistic license regularly.

ACKNOWLEDGMENTS

I would like to extend my sincere gratitude to the following people for their support in the writing of this book.

Michael Hauser
Martine Heines
Rick Heizman
Tom Lattanand
Piers Lawrence
Donna Moore

INTRODUCTION TO ALTERNATE TUNINGS

Why Use Alternate Tunings?

Let me start by saying that alternate tunings are by no means meant to be a substitute for standard tuning. They are apples and oranges, and useful for very different things. There is a lot of music for which standard tuning is the best possible choice. Gaining mastery over standard tuning can be a lifelong and ever-evolving quest and I'd encourage all serious players to continue to deepen their knowledge of it.

That said, alternate tunings open a whole new world of possibilities and allow us to play things that would be impossible in standard tuning. They allow for a resonance and richness in timbre that can only be achieved by making generous use of open strings. Generally, the longer the string length, the richer the sound and certainly the longer the sustain. Try playing the open high E string, then play E on the 2nd string, 5th fret, then play it on the 3rd string (9th fret), then the 4th (14th fret). With each successive E you get less and less sustain. Also, chord voicings that would be impossible in standard tuning become possible and sometimes even easy in another tuning. These voicings may contain tight intervals that spawn melodies out of picking patterns.

There are also many tunings that can greatly enhance the technique of tapping, by facilitating chord shapes that allow the necessary velocity of attack to be executed.

Track 1 - Standard Tuning

Alternate vs. Standard Tuning

There is a significant difference between the way we'll approach alternate tunings as compared to the way you've probably come to know standard tuning. The difference is generally based on the fact that in standard tuning, we are often required to play in multiple keys, and depending on what style we play, countless tonalities. In alternate tunings, however, we only need to know the key or keys that harmonize with the open strings. For this reason, the method for learning the fingerboard in an alternate tuning can be greatly simplified.

I have chosen to use DADGAD and other tunings where the three bass strings are tuned to root-5th-root to demonstrate the basic principles of this method.

This configuration allows for rich chordal shapes and gives us a consistent base from which to operate as we change the tuning of the top three strings. Although we'll be focusing mainly on root-5th-root-type tunings, the majority of what you'll learn in this book can be applied to any tuning.

SECTION ONE: THEORY ESSENTIALS

As I was first learning music theory, most of it happened in the context of studying jazz guitar. I was very fortunate to have a teacher, Michael DaRooge, who showed me in only a few lessons the building blocks I needed to continue progressing as a musician, regardless of whether or not I had a teacher.

Over the next few years, I found that each new tune or lick would expand my knowledge by allowing me a context in which to apply the theory I'd learned. Without a way to put theory to musical use, it is nothing more than math, and likely to be forgotten along with everything you learned in algebra class.

The foundation of diatonic harmony shown in this section is essential for understanding how to navigate through alternate tunings. If you find yourself getting bored or confused in learning the theory, take a break. Do something creative. Get out of the house if only long enough to work on that studio lounge tan. Listen to some music that inspires you.

If you haven't done so lately (or ever), listen to any of the ten volumes of Keith Jarrett's Sun Bear Concerts, all of which are improvised solo piano. The collection is a brilliant example of harmonic mastery put to soulful use. I am inspired every time I listen to it and continue to use it to learn new chord progressions and melodies.

① The Diatonic Chords

Having an understanding of basic diatonic harmony is fundamental to fretboard navigation in alternate tunings. The next two chapters should be thoroughly understood before looking at the alternate tunings in subsequent chapters. For this reason, all the examples in this chapter and the next are in standard tuning. If you already have a thorough understanding of diatonic harmony, you may want to skip this chapter.

Quite simply, diatonic harmony is any harmony based upon the whole step/half step pattern of a major scale. The steps are as follows:

W W h W W W h
1 2 3 4 5 6 7 1

The half step at the end is between the 7th degree and root of the next octave of the scale, where the sequence of whole and half steps may start again.

To see a visual representation of the major scale structure, play it entirely on one string. That way you can see, in a graphical way, the pattern of whole steps and half steps. This linear view is not commonly observed when learning scales on the guitar.

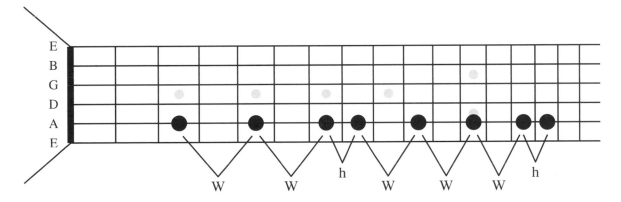

The easiest way to see the architecture of diatonic harmony is to look at it on the musical staff.

C Major Scale

1   2   3   4   5   6   7   1

Diatonic Triads over the C Major Scale

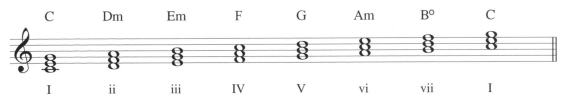

I   ii   iii   IV   V   vi   vii   I

There are seven notes in a major scale. You can form a chord on each of these notes by stacking notes in intervals of 3rds, as seen on the previous figure. These are the diatonic chords in the key of C. They are generally referred to by the Roman numerals as seen below the staff in the figure below. The Roman numerals are much more important than the chord letters for understanding how chords function and interact.

It's also vitally important to memorize the chord type for each of the seven chords. They are the same in every key. Notice that the I, IV, and V chords are major, the ii, iii, and vi chords are minor, and the vii chord is diminished. As shown here, the major chords are generally written in upper case while the minor and diminished chords are written in lower case. This is easy to remember. It's only seven chords. Learn them well! They comprise the framework of this entire system.

Now play this sequence in standard tuning so you can hear the harmony. These are the "stripped down" voicings, fingered here exactly as shown on the staff, wherein all the degrees of the chords move up together.

Using the chart "Diatonic Triads in All Keys" in the Reference Section, experiment with creating progressions from chords within a key. Listen to how well the chords within any given key go together. Note some of your favorite progressions, remembering them primarily by their Roman numerals, as opposed to their letter names.

Adding 7ths

We can take the harmony a step further now by adding 7ths to each of the seven diatonic triads. Notice that the IV major triad becomes a major seventh chord and the V chord becomes a dominant seventh (a major triad with an added ♭7). Also note that the vii diminished triad becomes a m7♭5 and not a diminished seventh chord.

C Major Scale

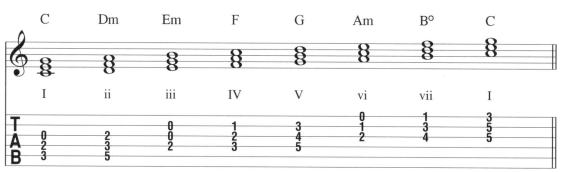

Diatonic 7th Chords over the C Major Scale

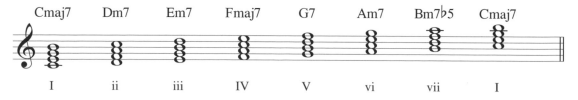

Here's a way you can play the sequence so that all the degrees of the chords move up together. The voicing (arrangement of notes in the chords) is 1–5–7–3.

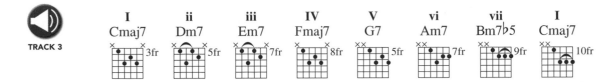

TRACK 3

Remember of course that the chord types are the same in every key. See "Diatonic Seventh Chords in All Keys" in the Reference section. As you did with the triads, experiment with creating progressions using chords within a key. Note some of your favorite progressions, remembering them by their Roman numerals, as opposed to their letter names. If you don't know how to play all these chords, don't worry; you can stick with the triads.

Although it is beyond the focus of this book to get any deeper into chord voicings in standard tuning, I would highly recommend that you continue to expand your standard tuning chordal vocabulary. Besides its obvious intrinsic value, much of what you learn in standard tuning can be utilized in alternate tunings.

In a chord progression, the key is determined by which scale all the chords have in common. For example, Emaj7 and Amaj7 are I and IV in the key of E. Key changes within a progression happen when a chord comes along that isn't found in the key established by the earlier chords.

➋
The Diatonic Modes

As we discussed in the previous chapter, a chord can be built on each of the seven notes in the major scale. Similarly, *modes* are scales created by using any one of the seven notes of the original major scale as the starting point, or tonic.

To keep the following figure simple and easy to read, only the first three modes are grouped in brackets.

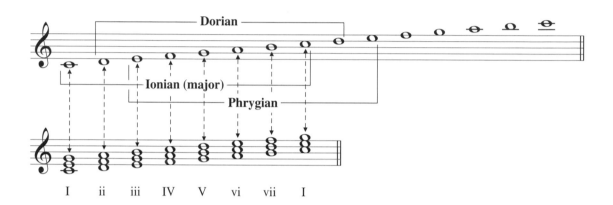

Each mode has a distinctly different sound and mood. Memorize all seven mode names until you know them like the back of your hand.

Diatonic Mode	Triad	Seventh Chord
I Ionian	C	Cmaj7
ii Dorian	Dm	Dm7
iii Phrygian	Em	Em7
IV Lydian	F	Fmaj7
V Mixolydian	G	G7
vi Aeolian	Am	Am7
vii Locrian	B°	Bm7♭5

Each of the modes corresponds to the chord based on the same root. Even though all seven modes are made up of the same notes, each one sounds unique because of its starting point, or tonic. When improvising or composing melody it is not necessary to start or stop all our phrases on the tonic in order to be "in the mode." That's determined by the chord or chords we're playing over. They create the tonal center against which we hear the mode. For example, if you're playing a phrase using notes in the C major scale over an Em chord, or even a drone on the low E string, your phrase will be heard in the Phrygian mode. Similarly, when playing the same phrase over a G chord, it will take on the sound of the G Mixolydian mode. If there is more than one chord in the progression, it is the chord with the most "tonal gravity" that determines the mode. The chord with the most tonal gravity is the one which sounds like it resolves the progression.

Common Chord Progressions and Their Modes

Here are a few common diatonic chord progressions with their tonic and mode. They are listed by Roman numeral only so that you can apply them to any key. They can be played as triads or seventh-type chords. If a chord progression sounds good played with triads it generally sounds good with the 7ths added. As an exercise, write out each of the progressions below in at least three different keys and play them. Listen to how they resolve to the tonic chord. You can use triads or seventh-type chords.

I   vi   ii   V
Tonic: I
Mode: Ionian (major)

ii   iii
Tonic: ii
Mode: Dorian

iii   IV
Tonic: iii
Mode: Phrygian

IV   V/IV
Tonic: IV
Mode: Lydian

V   IV
Tonic: V
Mode: Mixolydian

vi   ii
Tonic: vi
Mode: Aeolian (minor)

Derivative vs. Parallel

There are two fundamental ways of looking at the modes: *derivative* and *parallel*. So far we have viewed them only as derivative. In other words they were all derived from the same scale—D Dorian is derived from C major, E Phrygian is derived from C major, and so on. Seeing the modes as parallel is equally important and tells us infinitely more about why each mode sounds the way it does. To see the modes as parallel we look at each mode compared to the major scale of the same root, to see how they differ.

C Major	1	2	3	4	5	6	7
C Mixolydian	1	2	3	4	5	6	♭7
C Dorian	1	2	♭3	4	5	6	♭7

Here is a parallel view of all the modes listed in order of "brightness." A brighter scale is one with more sharps (or less flats).

1. Lydian	1	2	3	♯4	5	6	7
2. Ionian (major)	1	2	3	4	5	6	7
3. Mixolydian	1	2	3	4	5	6	♭7
4. Dorian	1	2	♭3	4	5	6	♭7
5. Aeolian (natural minor)	1	2	♭3	4	5	♭6	♭7
6. Phrygian	1	♭2	♭3	4	5	♭6	♭7
7. Locrian	1	♭2	♭3	4	♭5	♭6	♭7

Notice how with each successive mode you either take away a sharp or add a flat.

Play the low E string and let it sustain to create a drone, then starting on the open high E string, play the E Ionian mode (E major scale) on that string only. Spend some time improvising with it. Next do the same thing with each of the modes in the list. Notice how each mode gets progressively darker and has its own distinct sound and mood. Make sure you spend enough time with each mode to get an idea of its sound and mood.

③
Pentatonic Scales

The pentatonic scale is a five-note scale comprised of notes found in the diatonic scale. Within every diatonic key there are three major pentatonic scales, each with its own relative minor, making a total of six.

The pentatonic scale degrees are as follows.

Major Pentatonic	1	2	3	5	6
Minor Pentatonic	1	♭3	4	5	♭7

Every diatonic key also has three major chords and three minor chords, each with a corresponding pentatonic scale of the same root and major/minor identity. Here's what it all looks like in the key of C; each major is grouped with its relative minor.

Roman Numeral	Chords in C Grouped with Relative	Pentatonic Scale
I	C	C Major
vi	Am	A minor
IV	F	F Major
ii	Dm	D minor
V	G	G Major
iii	Em	E minor

Here's a basic pentatonic scale in standard tuning showing the major and relative minor roots.

Basic Pentatonic Scale in Standard Tuning

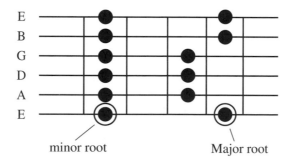

In almost all situations where a diatonic mode works, there will be at least one, and often two pentatonic scales, that also work.

The primary pentatonic is the one with the same root as the tonic chord and mode. For example, if the tonic chord is Cmaj7, the primary pentatonic is C. If the tonic chord is Em, the primary pentatonic is E minor.

The secondary pentatonic is generally found either a 4th or a 5th away. For major chords it often works out that the pentatonic scale based on the I chord is one of the two that work. So if the primary pentatonic is based on a IV or V chord, the secondary will be the one based on the I chord. If your primary pentatonic is based on a I chord, the secondary could be based on either the IV or the V, depending on the chords. You just have to try them and see which one fits.

For minor chords, finding pentatonic scales works the same way but with relative minors, i.e., vi is like I. ii and iii are like IV and V.

I've found the greatest use for the pentatonic scale in alternate tunings in the area of single note soloing, both in solo and ensemble contexts.

Using a pentatonic scale to solo in an alternate tuning should only be attempted if you've already been doing it for a while in standard tuning and know at least the basic fingering.

SECTION TWO: DADGAD

In this section we'll be focusing exclusively on the DADGAD tuning. Its harmonic flexibility and elements in common with standard tuning make it perfect for demonstrating our system of fretboard navigation. Later in the book, we'll use this system to map several other tunings, some with very different tonalities.

④

Tuning to DADGAD

As mentioned in the intro, we'll be using DADGAD to demonstrate the basic principles of alternate tuning navigation. This will not be an in-depth study of DADGAD, as that would require another book altogether.

The first rule of changing tunings is to get into the tuning before you start fine tuning. This is necessary because any time you tune a string by as much as a half step, it changes the tension on the neck slightly, thereby affecting the tuning of all the other strings.

Learn to be deadly accurate in your tuning. Listening to an out-of-tune guitar is about as much fun as being poked in the eye with a sharp stick. For more on the finer elements of tuning see Chapter 20, Tuning Tips.

Tuning to DADGAD *(from standard tuning)*

TRACK 4

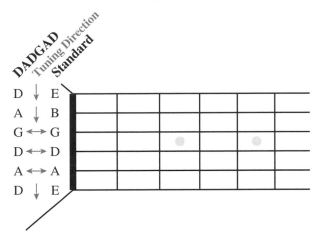

I use the 4th (D) string as the "home base" or reference pitch for tuning because it is close to the center of the guitar's pitch range, and because it functions as the root in many of the tunings I use.

Tuning Steps:

1. Tune both the 1st and 6th strings down a whole step to D, using the 4th string as a reference.

2. Tune the 2nd string down a whole step to A using the 5th string as reference. You should now be in DADGAD, but still need to fine tune.

3. Now we'll start to fine tune by repeating step 1, tuning both the 6th and 1st strings, one at a time, to the 4th string. If you have trouble accurately tuning octaves you can use harmonics to create a unison between the strings as follows:

   Tune the 1st string open to the 4th string, 12th fret harmonic.
   Tune the 6th string, 12th fret harmonic to the open 4th string.

4. Tune the 2nd string, 12th fret harmonic to the 4th string, 7th fret harmonic.

5. Tune the 5th string, 12th or 5th fret harmonic to the 4th string, 7th fret harmonic.

6. Tune the 3rd string, 7th fret harmonic to the 4th string, 5th or 12th fret harmonic.

7. In any tuning, it's a good idea to have a "tuning chord" to check your tuning that includes all six strings and is comprised solely of roots and 5ths.

In DADGAD, play all the open strings except for the 2nd fret on the 3rd string. These *power chords* with roots and 5ths only are generally named with the chord letter followed by 5; in this case, D5.

D5

NOTE: Major chords should never be used to check your tuning. This is because in the western world, we use the *tempered* system of tuning, which tunes the major 3rd slightly sharp from the natural harmonics of the overtone series. The result is that no major chord will ever sound really in tune. It's an unfortunate but necessary compromise employed to enable an instrument to play in all twelve keys without adjusting the tuning.

⑤

Fretboard Navigation in DADGAD

Let's start by looking at the tuning along with each note's scale degree.

$$\begin{array}{cccccc} \textbf{D} & \textbf{A} & \textbf{D} & \textbf{G} & \textbf{A} & \textbf{D} \\ 1 & 5 & 1 & 4 & 5 & 1 \end{array}$$

Notice how much repetition there is—three roots and two 5ths.

Unlike the way most of us learned to play in standard tuning, in this approach we'll be viewing the fingerboard lengthwise first, on one string at a time. You'll soon see how powerful this approach can be in quickly mapping out a tuning.

We'll start with the notes in the key of D major. The whole-step/half-step pattern of a major scale is WWhWWWh.

On the 4th string only, play a D major scale from the open string to fret 12.

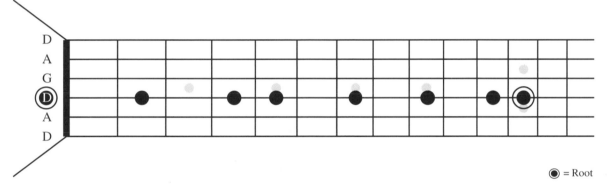

◉ = Root

Notice how easy it is to observe the whole-step/half-step pattern of the scale. Take a visual snapshot of the geometry of the pattern. Don't hesitate to use the fret markers as reference points. Burn it into your memory. It is the foundation of diatonic harmony and the methods of fretboard navigation used in this book.

On the following page are a couple of simple exercises that will help to solidify your muscle memory of this pattern.

> Most of the examples in this book should be played *sostenuto*. This means that you let all the notes of the chord sustain as long as possible, which is much longer than their exact written duration in the music. It would be a notation mess of dots and ties if it were indicated exactly how long each note should sustain. This way is much easier to read.
>
> Let each note ring as long as possible *until that string is needed again* for the same note or a different one. It's important to keep your left hand fingers down as long as you can but still get to the next chord on time. It's equally important not to damp the string by planting the right-hand fingers in advance of plucking.

> **NOTE:** The commonly-used fingerpicking symbols of *p-i-m-a* are used in the notation throughout to denote suggested right-hand fingerings:
>
> *p* = thumb (pulgar)   *i* = index (indicio)
> *m* = middle (medio)   *a* = ring (anular)

1. Using the right-hand pattern shown below, play the scale, ascending and descending.

Tuning:
(low to high) D-A-D-G-A-D

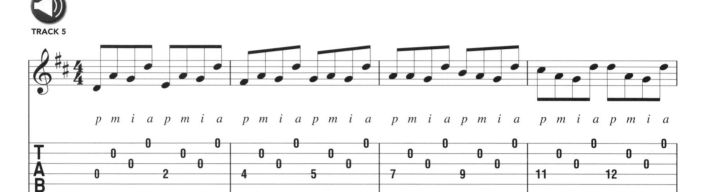

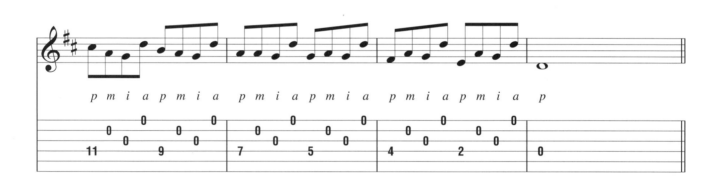

Next, using the same right-hand pattern, play the scale ascending and descending in 3rds.

Tuning:
(low to high) D-A-D-G-A-D

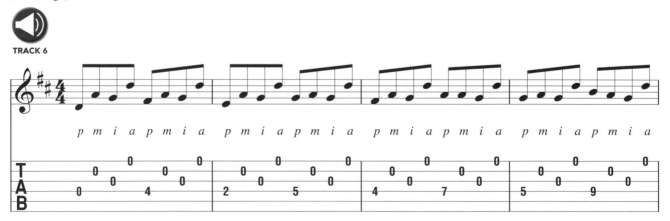

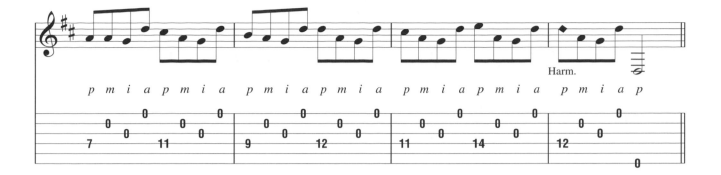

Remember, go at your own pace. Take as much time as you need to absorb the information and play each example in a relaxed way.

2. If you have the 4th string memorized, you're halfway there with the note mapping since the 1st and 6th strings are the same note as the 4th. Spend some time playing around on those strings to solidify your knowledge of the pattern.

3. Next go to the 5th string. This string is tuned to A, the 5th of the key, and the root (D) is located at the 5th fret. Starting at the 5th fret, play a D major scale, staying on the 5th string, ascending as high as you can comfortably go. Remember the major scale step pattern WWhWWWh. Now go back down the scale, continuing past where you started to include the degrees of the scale below the root. Notice that it's the same frets as on the 4th string with only one exception at the 10th fret.

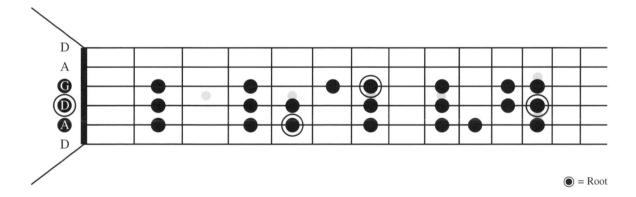

⦿ = Root

> When playing in a major scale or any of its modes, there will only be one spot where the frets for that scale differ between two strings tuned a 4th or a 5th apart. Most alternate tunings have multiple occurrences of this string relationship, so it's important to remember this rule. It will go a long way towards simplifying your view of the fingerboard.

4. Finally, play the D major scale on the 3rd string, starting at fret 7 as shown above. Play as high as you can comfortably reach and then descend to the open G. Notice how this string's pattern only differs from the D string's pattern in one place: at the 6th fret.

6

Thirds Expanded in DADGAD

This chapter assumes that you've spent some time absorbing the previous two chapters or you already have a solid understanding of the basic principles of diatonic harmony. We're going to look at a method of creating the diatonic chords in D using only the root and the 3rd of each chord. We'll be starting on the 4th and 5th strings. These strings are the same pitches in DADGAD as in standard tuning and the following shapes are used all the time in standard tuning in nearly every style. You may already be familiar with them, though it's still a good idea to spend some time playing in DADGAD to hear how they interact with the open strings.

An Important Word About Open Strings

Throughout this book you'll find many new chord sets like the ones below. It's important to play each series a couple of times just as written, without including any extra open strings. However, one of the greatest assets of playing in alternate tunings is that we generally play in keys of which the open strings are a part. This allows them to harmonize nicely with most of the diatonic chords in that key. Strings tuned to the root or 5th almost always will harmonize, and strings tuned to the 4th and other scale degrees often will harmonize. As the open strings remain static and the chords move around, the open strings will have various effects on the type of chord produced. They may act as a 9th and 13th over one chord and as 5th and 9th over another. The point is that the chord will function the same way as in its simple form. That is to say a I chord is still a I chord, V is still V, and so on. The real magic of a tuning is engaged largely by making use of the open strings.

We'll start by playing the root (D) at the 5th string, 5th fret, and its major 3rd on the 4th fret of the 4th string. This forms the I chord. These two notes are all that are required to define the chord.* From here we'll create the rest of the chords, I through vii, as seen below. We can call these voicings *low root closed*.

These terms mean:
1. The chord is based on a low string (string 5)
2. The chord is in *root position*, meaning the root is on the bottom of the voicing
3. The voicing is *closed*, meaning the chord tones (root and 3rd in this case) are as close together as possible.

Low Root Closed Voicings

*The 5th, unless flattened or sharped, is not generally required to define the identity of a chord.

Notice how the shape for a major chord is a one-fret spacing and the shape for a minor chord is two frets. The I, IV, and V are of course major, and the ii, iii, and vi chords are minor. The vii chord is also just a minor shape in this case. (Although the vii chord is a diminished chord, the ♭5 is the only note that distinguishes it from a minor chord, and there are no 5ths in these voicings.)

Here's a simple exercise that will help you solidify the pattern. As the pattern becomes familiar to your muscle memory, be sure to stay aware of which chord you're on, even as the pattern becomes second nature. Be sure to always identify the chords by their Roman numerals. The letter name is usually only important if you're writing out charts for other instrumentalists. Feel free to use any right-hand picking pattern you like, as long as you cover all the chords.

Tuning:
(low to high) D-A-D-G-A-D

TRACK 7

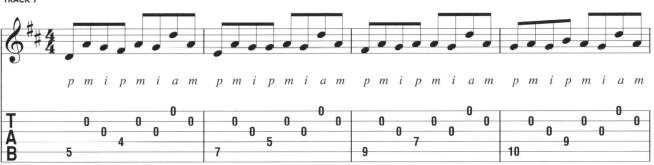

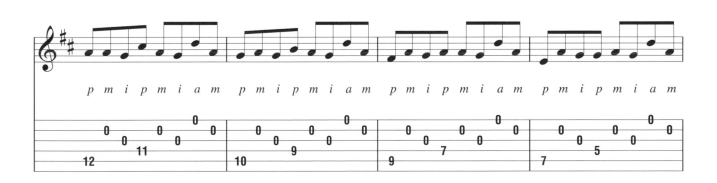

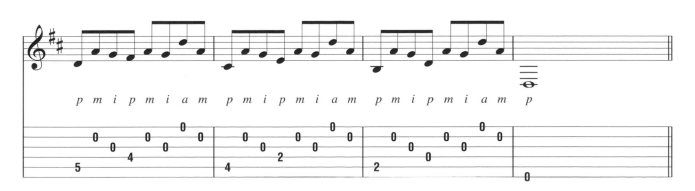

Now here's where all the repetition of open-string pitches in DADGAD really comes in handy. In a *high root closed* voicing, the 1st and 2nd strings are the same pitches as the 4th and 5th, so you can take the whole thing up an octave without learning any new shapes: a dream come true for the lazy.

High Root Closed Voicings

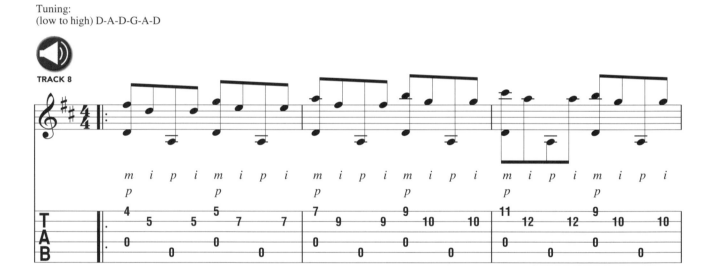

Here's a simple exercise that will help you continue solidifying these shapes.

Tuning:
(low to high) D-A-D-G-A-D

TRACK 8

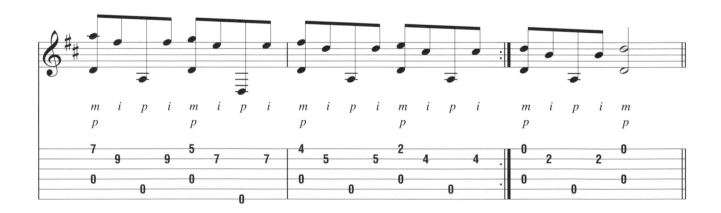

22

Next we'll take the root from the low set and the 3rd from the high set. These are the same shapes as the original, only spread out, so now you're playing 10ths. These voicings are very rich when embellished with the open strings.

Low Root Open Voicings

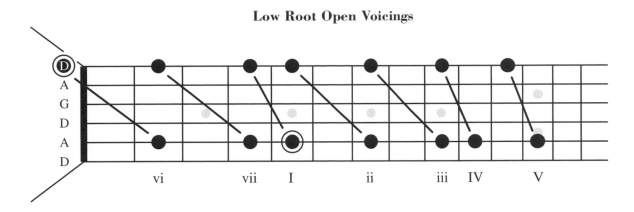

Here's an exercise that makes use of the aforementioned open strings.

Tuning:
(low to high) D-A-D-G-A-D

TRACK 9

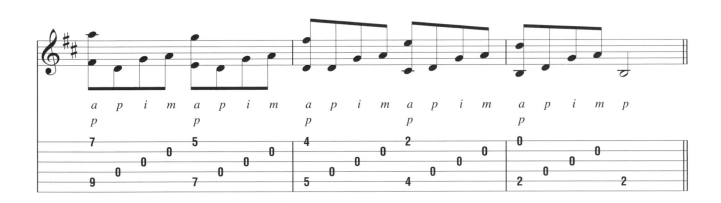

Now we'll keep the root from the low set but play the 3rd down an octave, on the 6th string. These are the same chords as the original, consisting of roots and 3rds, but now they're *inverted*, resulting in 6ths.

In order to keep your bearings when playing these, be sure to stay focused on the 5th string. Although it's the higher note of the pair, it is the root and dictates the name and function of the chord in this context.

Low Root Inverted Voicings

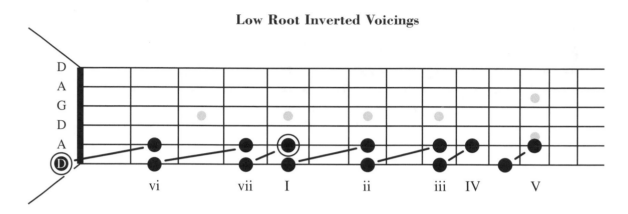

In this exercise we hear the richness of 6ths in the lower register of the guitar.

Tuning:
(low to high) D-A-D-G-A-D

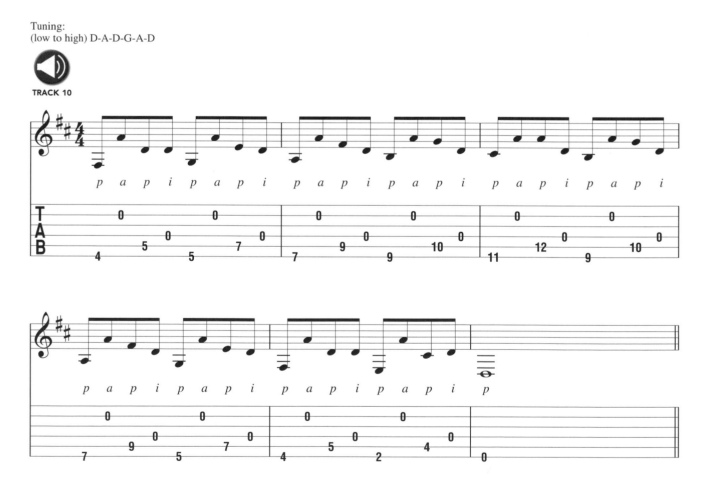

TRACK 10

Lastly, we'll take the root from the high set and play the 3rd from the low set. Again, these are the same chords as the original set, only inverted, resulting in 6ths. In order to keep your bearings, be sure to stay focused on the 2nd string. Although it's the higher of the pair, it is the root and dictates the name and function of the chord in this context.

High Root Inverted Voicings

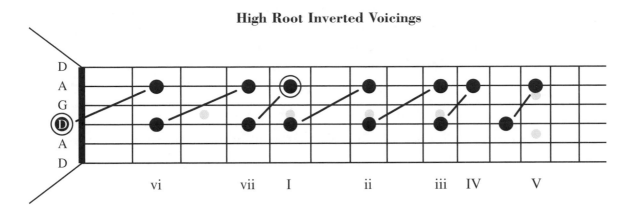

Here's an exercise using the above configuration. Stay focused on the higher note of each pair. Before moving on to the next chapter, make sure you have a good handle on these shapes.

Tuning:
(low to high) D-A-D-G-A-D

TRACK 11

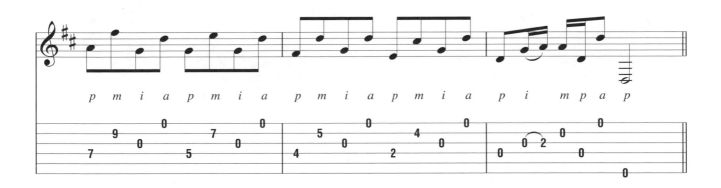

7
DADGAD Bass Triads

In this chapter we're going to cover a set of chord voicings played on the three bass strings in DADGAD tuning. They are simply the diatonic triads in D major using a voicing of 1–5–3, but using *first inversion* I and V chords for iii and vii. These very common chord substitutions flow nicely into the next chord and tend to harmonize with the open strings of most diatonic tunings more easily than iii and vii. We will notate them as follows: I/3 and V/7.

For a detailed explanation of the iii and vii chord substitutions, see page 28.

For a detailed explanation of the iii and vii chord substitutions, see page 28.

Diatonic Triads in D Major *(DADGAD)*

TRACK 12

I	ii	iii(+5)	IV	V	iv	vii(+5)	I
D	Em	D/F♯	G	A	Bm	A/C♯	D
4fr		4fr	5fr	7fr	9fr	11fr	12fr
		I/3				V/7	

Notice in the pictures below how the first finger is bent back slightly to cover the 5th and 6th strings, while leaving the 1st, 2nd, and 3rd strings open. For some, it's easy to bend that joint backwards enough to execute this chord. If you find the chord difficult at first, try angling the first finger back a little or tipping it on its side a bit. You'll get it. Just keep working on it.

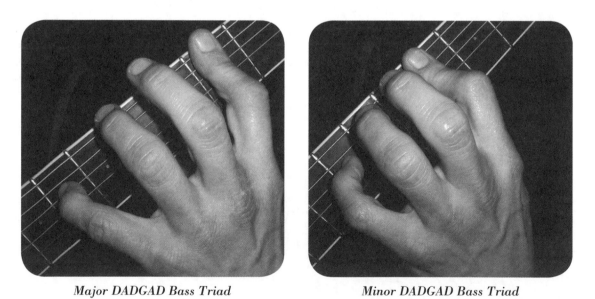

Major DADGAD Bass Triad   *Minor DADGAD Bass Triad*

Play through the chords using the bass strings only a few times, to make sure you're playing them cleanly. Then try adding the top three open strings. You can use the picking pattern on Track 13 on the following page or any other simple six-string picking pattern. Play with these chords until it becomes easy.

26

The chord names given are based on the lower three strings only. In most cases you'll want to include the open strings for the richness they add, but note that the open G string in DADGAD can clash with the iii or the first-inversion I chord (D/F#) in the key of D and should be avoided unless it's used just before changing to another chord.

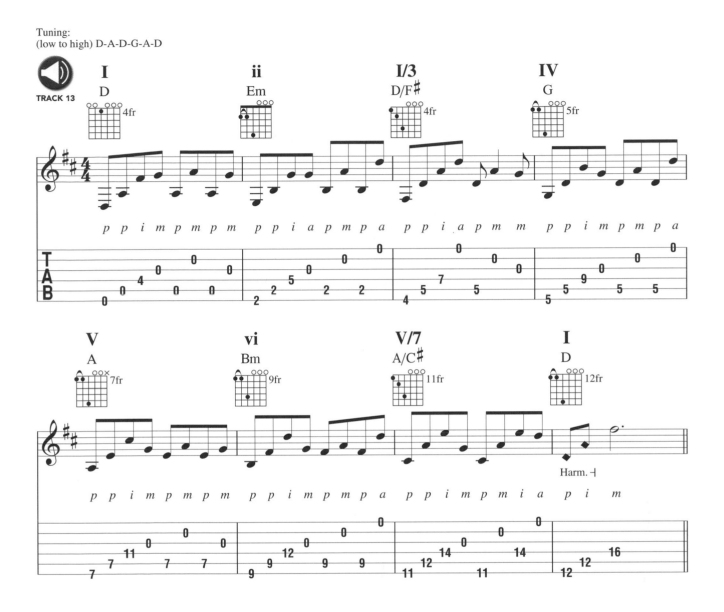

Remember to think of the chords primarily by their Roman numerals and chord type (major, minor, etc.), as this is the structure on which the entire diatonic system is based. For now, the letter names are much less important in understanding the theory.

Following are some common diatonic chord progressions. Using the voicings we just learned with any simple six-string picking pattern, play through each of them until you become familiar with its sound. Associate the Roman numeral for each chord with its respective scale step.

Common Diatonic Chord Progressions

1. | vi | | IV | |
2. | I | | IV | |
3. | ii | I/3 | IV | |
4. | ii | V | I | |
5. | I | vi | ii | V |

Make sure you understand the theory behind the iii and vii chord variations, as we'll use them again.

The iii Chord Substitution

Using the I/3 (the I chord with its 3rd in the bass) instead of the iii chord creates a rich voicing that flows nicely into the IV and many other places. Another convenient way of seeing this chord is as if you were raising the 5th of the iii chord (voiced 1–5–3).

$$I/3 = iii(+5)$$

This variation is not used if the iii chord happens to be functioning as the tonic: a "Phrygian" modal chord progression.

The vii Chord Substitution

The diatonic triad on step vii is diminished, containing $1-\flat3-\flat5$. Often we substitute a V chord in first inversion for the vii chord. In classical theory, V and vii are said to be in the same chord *family*, the dominant family. With an inverted V, we get a very warm-sounding chord that still seeks resolution like the vii chord, but is a little less dissonant. It's important to understand that the vii chord functions much like a V chord.

$$V/7 = vii(+5)$$

The V/7 voicing is explored in greater depth in Chapter 13, "Creating Modulation."

⑧
The Half-Barre Bass

The half-barre bass is played using the first finger to barre the bottom three strings while leaving the top three open. This requires your finger to bend backwards a little at the first joint.

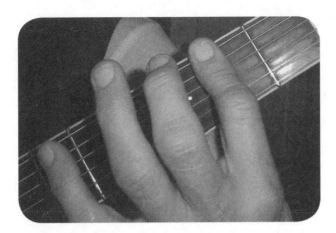

If you've learned the bass triads in the previous chapter, this shape shouldn't be too difficult. It just tends to be slightly harder since now you have to cover the 4th string as well the 5th and 6th. As with any chord that's hard to play at first (or even if it seems impossible), it'll become easier if you keep trying it every day for several weeks. Try angling the finger back a little or tipping it on its side a bit. You don't have to be double-jointed to play it.

In DADGAD and other 1–5–1 based tunings, this barre provides the 1–5–1 foundation on which a wide range of chords can be built, including the triads from the last chapter. Because it's played using only the first finger, the other fingers are free to play basslines, melodies, inner-voice movements and more. Its all-on-one-fret configuration makes it possible to do powerful hammer-ons and pull-offs to and from the shape.

The following exercise will help you to strengthen the first finger as well as solidify your fretboard knowledge in DADGAD or any other tuning with a 1–5–1 bass.

With the half barre as its foundation, this exercise creates middle- and lower-voice movement, utilizing notes in the key that are reachable from the barre.

Be sure to take advantage of the opportunity in the last two measures to release the barre momentarily. Without a break from the half barre, the left hand gets tired very quickly.

The half-barre is used first over the ii chord, then over the IV chord, but it can and should be practiced on any of the diatonic bass chords whose foundation is the half barre. For the major key, that would include V and vi, in addition to the I and IV shown here. Note that all four follow the same scale pattern.

The ii Chord

Tuning:
(low to high) D-A-D-G-A-D

The IV Chord

Tuning:
(low to high) D-A-D-G-A-D

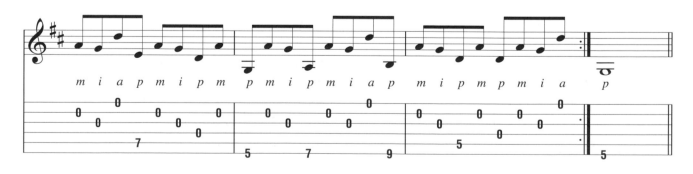

30

9

Finding Modes and Chords in DADGAD

In this chapter, we'll cover a method to determine which modes we can use in a tuning. We'll continue using DADGAD for now to demonstrate the basic fret mapping technique, although this method works for any diatonic tuning. Use these three steps to find the correct mode for a tuning.

1. **Name the chord formed by the open strings.**

    (For help, see "Chord Construction" in the Reference Section.)

    In the case of DADGAD, the chord is Dsus4.

2. **Determine this chord's possible diatonic function(s).**

    (For help, consult the following charts in the Reference Section: "Diatonic Triads," "Diatonic Seventh Chords," or "Extended Diatonic Chord Functions.")

    Dsus4 may function as I, ii, iii, V or vi.

    The possible modes are those that correspond to the chord numbers: the first, second, third, fifth, and sixth modes. These are Ionian (major), Dorian, Phrygian, Mixolydian, or Aeolian (natural minor).

3. **Test a mode by playing up and down on a root string while fingerpicking on the open strings.**

    Listen to how the mode works against the open strings.

> **IMPORTANT:** There are times when one of the "usable" modes really just doesn't sound that great over the tuning. This is usually due to the voicing created by the open strings. Sometimes one string will clash with the mode, especially when it's played as often as is an open string. Always let your ear be your guide.

We've already covered the basics of Ionian (the major scale) in previous chapters, so we'll look at the remaining four possibilities.

You can map out any new mode derivatively, using the same pattern as the major scale (W–W–h–W–W–W–h), but shifting it so that the first degree of the desired mode falls on the open string. Then find the fret where this puts the major scale root and use it as a point of reference to see the familiar pattern of whole steps and half steps.

For example, to map the Mixolydian mode, start by designating one of the root strings as the 5th degree of the major scale. For DADGAD, we can use string 1, 4, or 6. Let's use string 6.

Since Mixolydian is mode number five, it corresponds to the 5th degree of the major scale. From 5 to 6 in the scale is a whole step. From 6 to 7 is another whole step (two frets higher still). The final half step from 7 to 8 puts the root note (I) of a major scale at the 5th fret (the circled dot in the figure below). Familiarize yourself with this new perspective by playing up and down the string until you recognize the pattern.

This principle applies to all the strings because the fretboard pattern is the same as the major scale, but shifted five frets higher. We've already mapped out the major scale in Chapter 5, "Fretboard Navigation in DADGAD." Below is the Mixolydian fret map for DADGAD.

DADGAD Mixolydian Mode

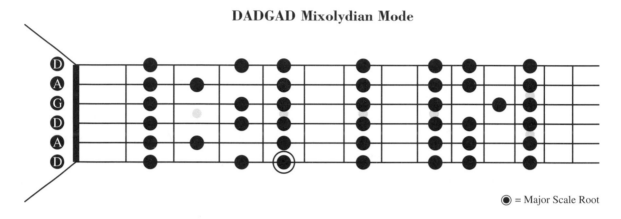

⊙ = Major Scale Root

It's important to understand that this major-scale derivative view of the mode is just the first stage of a more complete understanding that should also include a parallel view: seeing and hearing the intervals of the mode from its root. The derivative perspective is good for getting your fingers quickly into familiar patterns, and the parallel perspective is best for understanding what makes each mode sound the way it does.

In the derivative view, D Mixolydian is the fifth mode of a G major scale.

In the parallel view, D Mixolydian mode is compared to D major. There is only one note that is different: D Mixolydian has a ♭7th: a C♮ instead of C♯.

The following fretboard maps illustrate the remaining usable modes in DADGAD. The open D string is the mode's tonic and the major scale root is circled.

DADGAD Dorian Mode

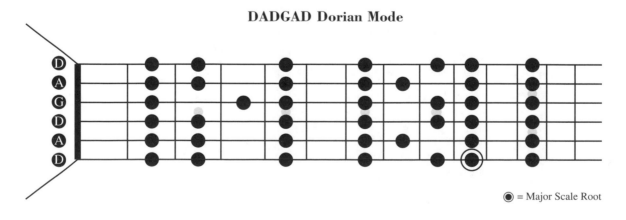

⊙ = Major Scale Root

DADGAD Aeolian Mode

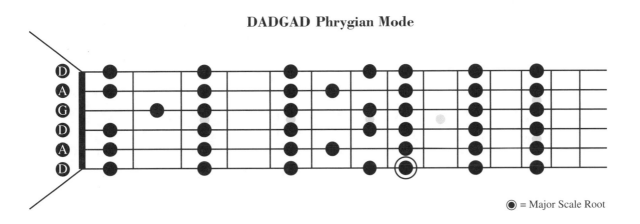

⦿ = Major Scale Root

DADGAD Phrygian Mode

⦿ = Major Scale Root

If you already know your diatonic scale fingerings in standard tuning (EADGBE), remember that the 3rd, 4th, and 5th strings (G, D, and A) are the same in DADGAD, so take advantage of fingerings you already know. Whatever approach you take to note mapping in a new mode or key, it takes a lot of playing in that mode and in that tuning to really burn it into the memory so it becomes second nature.

Now we're ready to map out the bass triads that are used to create the modal environment. We'll start with Mixolydian. We know the V chord is major, so now play the major shape as in the first chord below. That being the V chord, we'll now find the I chord at the 5th fret. Notice how it's the same set of chord shapes as the major set from the previous chapter, but with a new starting place. The chord names represent the fretted tones only, while the indicated open strings can be added for embellishment.

Mixolydian Chords in DADGAD

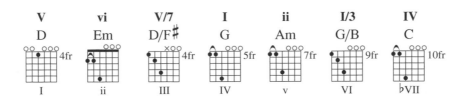

Each set of chords we'll cover here will be the same set, in the same order, differing only in its starting place.

The Roman numerals above the chord boxes represent the derivative view and the ones below represent the parallel view.

Next let's look at Dorian, the second mode. We know the ii chord is minor, so now play the minor shape as in the first chord below. Since we're calling that the ii chord, just for the purpose of finding the related major scale, we now find the I chord of that major key at the 10th fret.

Dorian Chords in DADGAD

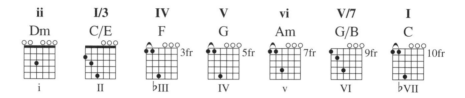

Beneath the grids the chords are labeled from the parallel point of view. The i chord in a Dorian modal center is minor, ii is also minor, the ♭III is major, and so on. Notice that we can still use the inverted substitutes from the original major key that we studied: C/E and G/B. This time they're subbing for ii and vi.

Now let's find the chords for Aeolian (natural minor), the sixth mode. We start by calling the open bass string, D, the 6th degree of a major scale. We know the vi chord is minor, so now play the minor shape as shown below. Since we're calling that the vi chord, we now find the I chord at the 3rd fret.

Aeolian Chords in DADGAD

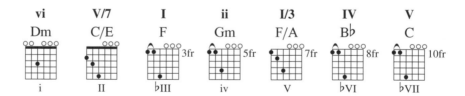

Last but not least is Phrygian, the third mode. First we'll call the open bass string, D, the 3rd of a B♭ major scale. We know the iii chord is minor, so now play the minor shape as in the first chord shown below. Since we're calling that the iii chord, we now find the related I chord at the 8th fret. Note that when the iii chord is the tonic, the 5th is not raised to create the I/3 substitute used in the other modes.

Phrygian Chords in DADGAD

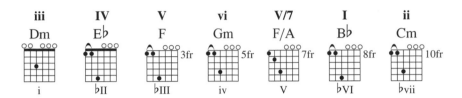

EXERCISE: Take a picking pattern you want to practice, and play it over some chords in the new mode. As always, it's important to think of the chords by their numeric names, and associate this with the sound of the progression. The numbers at the bottom of the previous diagrams indicate chord functions within the given mode.

SECTION THREE: BEYOND DADGAD

As we explore some new tunings in the next few chapters, we'll be using the same basic method of navigation as we did for DADGAD. Be sure you've absorbed the previous chapters and understand the concept of derivative and parallel views of the modes.

Most of the tunings I use have a 1–5 or a 1–5–1 configuration in the bass, in which the three bottom strings are tuned in the relationship of root-5th-root. I've found that ultimately, this allows me much greater freedom of expression than I'd have if I were to change the entire tuning in search of a new sound. The bass strings provide a consistent chordal platform from which to navigate, while the vast array of upper string combinations allows for nearly any tonality to be created.

There are, of course, countless great tunings with different bass configurations. I love to experiment with new tunings and encourage you to do the same, but if you learn this system of navigation focusing on 1–5–1 based tunings, you'll be able to apply its method in any tuning.

⑩
Mapping the D7sus4 Tuning

D A D G C D
1 5 1 4 ♭7 1

The only change in this tuning from DADGAD is the 2nd string, but it definitely changes the character of the tuning. The ♭7 tends to give it a little more edge.

To determine the modes that work, we'll go through the three-step process outlined in Chapter 9.

1. Name the chord formed by the open strings.
(For help see "Chord Construction" in the Reference section.)

The chord created by DADGCD is D7sus4.

2. Determine this chord's possible diatonic function(s), e.g., I, IV, V.
(For help, consult the following charts in the Reference section: "Diatonic Triads," "Diatonic Seventh Chords," or "Extended Diatonic Chord Functions.")

The D7sus4 chord can function as ii, iii, V, or vi.

The usable modes are those that correspond to the chords based on those numbers.

> ii — D Dorian is equal to C major.
> iii — D Phrygian is equal to B♭ major.
> V — D Mixolydian is equal to G major.
> vi — D Aeolian is equal to F major.

3. Test a mode by playing up and down on a root string while fingerpicking on some open strings.

Listen to how it works against the open strings.

Now let's look at the fretboard maps of these modes. We mapped all four of them in DADGAD in the previous chapter. The only difference here is the 2nd string. It is the ♭7th, so the tonic can be found a whole step up, on the 2nd fret. You can use that as a reference point to get your bearings. Following are the fret maps for the four diatonic modes that work in DADGCD.

DADGCD Mixolydian Mode

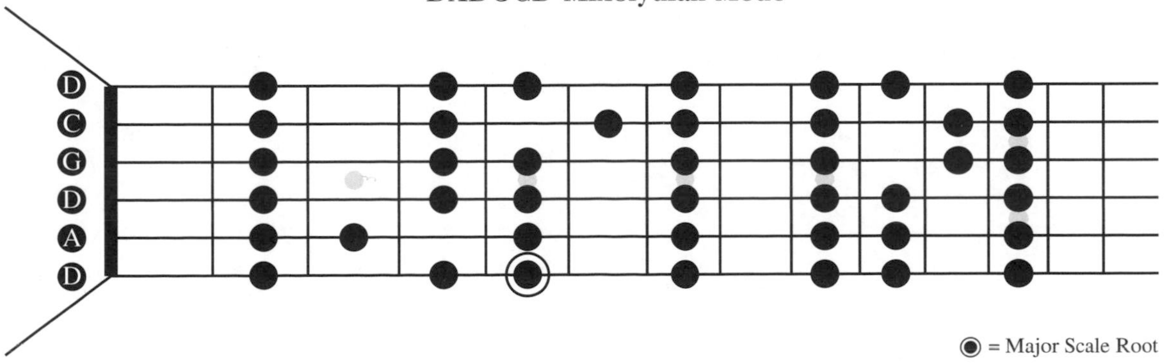

◉ = Major Scale Root

DADGCD Dorian Mode

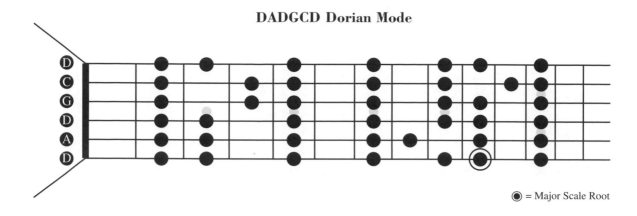

⊙ = Major Scale Root

DADGCD Aeolian Mode

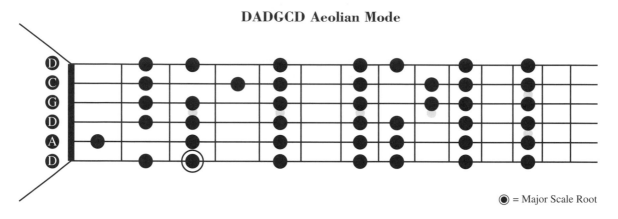

⊙ = Major Scale Root

DADGCD Phrygian Mode

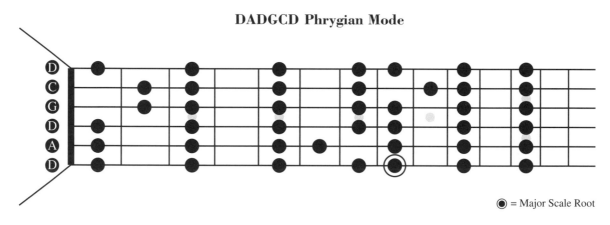

⊙ = Major Scale Root

To get deeper into a mode, learn the diatonic bass triads. See "Diatonic Bass Triads for 1–5–1 Tunings" in the Reference section for the corresponding bass triads.

Pick a mode you like, and spend some time getting familiar with its sound and fingerings in the tuning. Remember that many fingerings that work in DADGAD also work in this tuning. Also remember that on the 2nd string, the root is now located at the 2nd fret.

If you want to work on some new picking patterns while learning a tuning, check out Chapter 16, "Picking Patterns and Excerpts."

Shifting the Tonic

Although we've been using an open root string such as the 6th string as a point of reference to map out a tuning, it may not necessarily be the tonic. In this chapter we'll examine a new tuning and look at part of a piece that demonstrates this concept. The tuning is:

$$\begin{array}{cccccc} \mathbf{D} & \mathbf{A} & \mathbf{D} & \mathbf{G^{\sharp}} & \mathbf{A} & \mathbf{E} \\ 1 & 5 & 1 & {}^{\sharp}4 & 5 & 9 \end{array}$$

The open strings of this tuning form the chord Dsus2♯11, which can function only as a IV chord, due to the presence of the ♯11. Therefore, Lydian is the only mode that will work in this tuning when using the open D string as the tonic.

In using this tuning to illustrate the concept of the tonic being a note other than an open root string, I want to make it clear that you can do this in any tuning. There's nothing about this tuning that makes it better suited than any other to shift the tonic. I just chose this one because the piece we'll be drawing from is in this tuning.

This tuning works great for playing in D Lydian, but like any tuning, you could establish the tonic around any number of the other chords in the same key. Such is the case in my piece, "Faster Than Alone" from *Vanishing Borders*.

In the main chord progression, the vi chord, located at the 4th fret, is actually the tonic. Although it still makes sense to use the open 6th string and Lydian mode fretboard map as a point of reference, understand that in this case, it's only a fingering reference. The tonic chord actually dictates the mode in which we hear the progression, although the fretboard map stays the same. The main progression is vi–I–IV–V, which clearly resolves to the vi chord. This puts us in Aeolian or natural minor. When analyzed from the Aeolian perspective, the progression is i–♭III–♭VI–♭VII in the minor key.

Note that "Faster Than Alone" makes occasional use of the raised 7th and also includes a bridge section (not shown here) that goes through a number of key changes before coming back to this key.

What follows is the main A section chord vamp. There are two versions here. The first is the chord progression with simple fingerpicking, so you can quickly learn it to hear the chordal movement and tonic. The second version is the actual strum/picking pattern I use in playing the piece. I've included this for those who might want to learn the groove. The important thing, however, is to fingerpick through the chord progression to get a sense of the chord movement and tonic.

Faster Than Alone
A Section Chord Vamp - (Simple Picking)

Tuning:
(low to high) D-A-D-G♯-A-E

TRACK 16

Faster Than Alone
Strum/Picking Rhythm

Tuning:
(low to high) D-A-D-G♯-A-E

TRACK 17

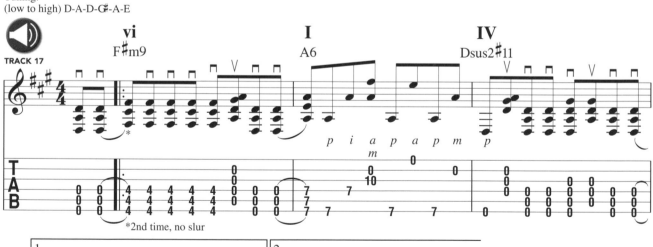

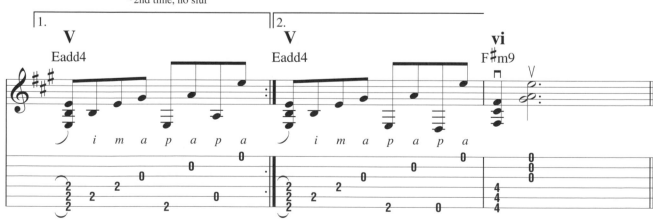

12

E-Based Tunings

In this chapter we'll be looking at two tunings with E as their root and 6th string. Now that our root is a whole step higher than it was in DADGAD, you can see the importance of knowing the diatonic chords by their Roman numerals. The fact that we're up a whole step has no effect on the functioning of the diatonic system.

Also remember that the bass triad voicings we used in the D-based tunings work universally among tunings with 1–5–1 in the bass. This means you can use the appropriate chord sets from the "Diatonic Bass Triads for 1–5–1 Tunings" chart in the Reference section for both tunings in this chapter when you want to quickly find some voicings that will create a specific modal environment.

The first tuning we'll look at is E–B–E–F♯–B–E.

E	B	E	F♯	B	E
1	5	1	9	5	1

This is one of the first alternate tunings I explored, having seen it listed on the back of Alex DeGrassi's *Slow Circle* album. It was in this tuning that I developed much of the foundation for the system I still use to map tunings. Like DADGAD, this tuning is harmonically flexible and facilitates many rich chord voicings with relatively easy fingerings.

Other than being up a whole step, this tuning differs from DADGAD only in that the 3rd string is a 9th or 2nd degree, instead of a 4th. The chord formed by the open strings is Esus2, consisting of roots, 5ths, and a 2nd. The usable modes are Ionian, Dorian, Mixolydian, and Aeolian. Although Lydian would theoretically work over an Esus2 chord, the ♯4 it contains can clash with some of the open strings in this tuning.

I use this tuning on the chord part in "Sun & Water" from my first album, *Aqua Touch*. It's also found on the first *Windham Hill Guitar Sampler*. This was one of my first compositions and was originally recorded with both guitars in standard tuning.

It would be another couple of years before I started playing in alternate tunings, arranging the chord part in E–B–E–F♯–B–E to discover a richness in the voicings that would be impossible in standard tuning. Its main chord progression revolves around C♯ minor, the relative minor of E major, and is a good example of the root of the tuning not being the tonic of a chord progression.

For both sections, use this picking pattern except where indicated:

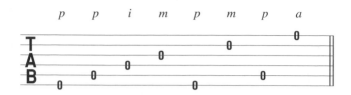

Sun & Water
First Half

Tuning:
(low to high) E-B-E-F#-B-E

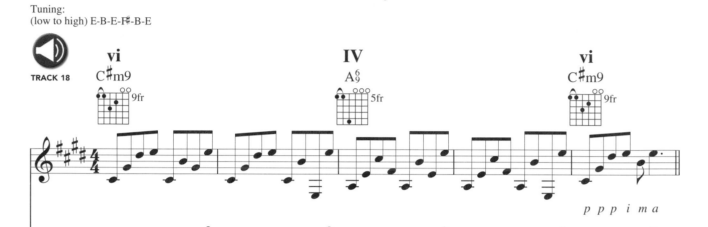

Sun & Water
Second Half

Tuning:
(low to high) E-B-E-F#-B-E

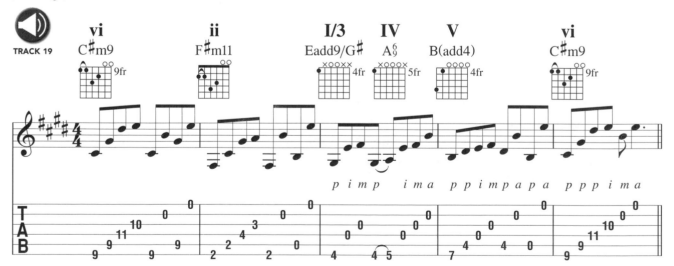

One of the things I like about tunings voiced 1–5–1–9 in the bottom four strings like this one is that it makes it easy to add a 9th to many of the diatonic bass triads. Here are the shapes for both major and minor add9 chords.

maj(add9)   m(add9)

In these voicings, we use the 3rd string to play the 3rd of the chord, and the 4th string to play the 9th. Providing possibilities to be used in various keys, the major chord shape harmonizes nicely with the open strings when played at frets 1, 3, 5, 7, 8, and 10, as will the minor shape at frets 2, 5, 7, 9, and 12.

Remember, much of what we did in DADGAD will work in this tuning. Use the similarities to your advantage in getting to know the tuning.

The next tuning changes only the top two strings but creates a very different harmonic landscape.

E	B	E	F♯	A	D
1	5	1	9	4	♭7

These notes form a 9sus4 chord, which can function as ii, V, or vi, depending on the surrounding chords and melodic content. As explained in Chapter 9, "Finding Modes and Chords in DADGAD," there are times when one of the theoretically usable modes really just doesn't sound good over the tuning. This is usually due to the voicing created by the open strings.

In this case, our modal options are really only Dorian and Aeolian. Although Mixolydian usually works very well over a 9sus4 chord, it does not sound good against this tuning due to its voicing. This tuning really wants to be treated like a minor chord, even though no minor 3rd is present.

I use this tuning for the chord part on the title track of my CD *One Heart Wild*. It's based around E Dorian, with the bridge shifting the tonality to B Aeolian. Note that this is not really a key change since both modes derive from the D major scale. All strums are played with the first finger of the right hand unless otherwise indicated. Up and downstrokes are shown between staves with arrows.

One Heart Wild
First Section

Tuning:
(low to high) E-B-E-F#-A-D

TRACK 20

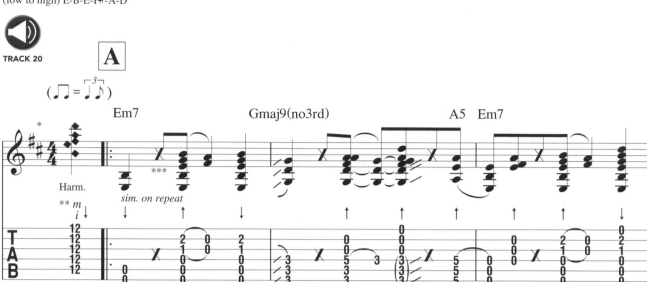

*Key signature denotes E Dorian.
  **Flick right-hand index and middle fingers downward across strings in rapid succession.
    ***Slap strings percussively with knuckles of right hand.

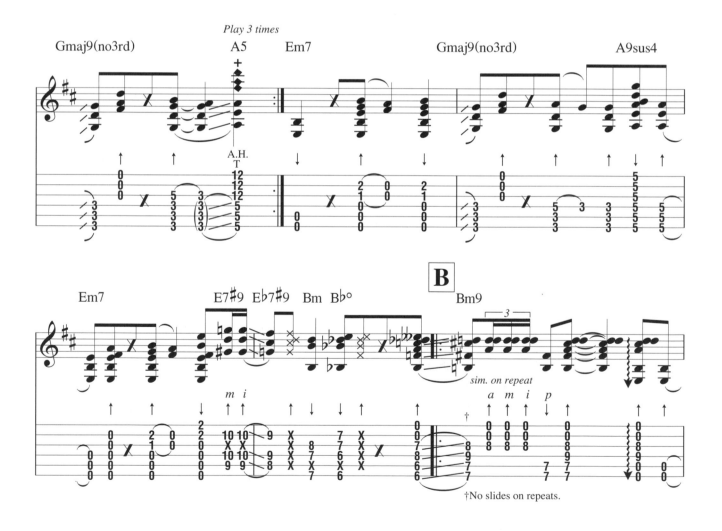

†No slides on repeats.

SECTION FOUR: BEYOND DIATONIC

13
Creating Modulation

One of the great things about alternate tunings is that they can facilitate chordal richness, much of which is provided by generous use of the open strings. While this is generally desirable and in large part the reason for using alternate tunings, it can also at times start to sound a little "dronish."

Often a *modulation*—moving out of the established key—can stimulate the ear and allow a return to the original key with a newfound freshness. Leaving the key is obviously not difficult. The trick is to do it gracefully.

The two basic elements of modulation are harmonic (chordal) and melodic. Either can work independently, but are most often used together, with the harmony being the driving force. While rhythm can play a role in a successful modulation, it does so as an aspect of harmony or melody.

Modulating permanently to a key that is radically different from the one you started in generally defeats the purpose of using an open tuning, since the open strings aren't likely to be harmonious in both keys. Therefore we'll focus first on modulations that venture out of the key for only one chord at a time, and next on some where we move to another tonal center for longer, but eventually return. In either case, modulation is generally done via the V chord of the new key.

The V Chord and Its Disguises

- The V is built on a major triad, and often includes a ♭7. The classical name for the 5th scale degree and its accompanying chord is the *dominant*.
- The V chord creates a relative tension that seeks resolution to its tonic chord, usually I (major key) or i (minor key).
- It may have a suspended 4th.
- It may contain any of the following degrees: 9th, 11th, or 13th, as well as ♭5th, ♯5th, ♭9th, or ♯9th.
- It may be inverted, having any chord tone or any of the aforementioned extensions or alterations in the bass.

With all these versions of the V chord possible, there are countless ways of using it to create modulations. We'll look first at its role in what's called a *secondary dominant chord* to twist the harmony slightly and then resolve to another chord in the key.

Secondary Dominant Chords

Each of the seven diatonic chords except I and vii has its own V chord which is known as its secondary dominant. A momentary modulation can be created by going to the secondary dominant of any of these chords and then resolving to it. For example, the diatonic ii chord in the key of C is Dm. The V of that chord is A7. This chord is labeled the V7/ii ("five of two"). There are five secondary dominant chords in any major key: V/ii, V/iii, V/IV, V/V, and V/vi.

Although secondary dominant chords do contain notes that fall outside of the original key, they are heard as chromatic passing tones and thereby retain the sound of the original key.

Often, simply moving one of the voices of a diatonic chord up or down can create a modulation by turning it into a V chord of another chord, to which it then can resolve. In the case of secondary dominants, these targets of resolution are other chords in the same key. You may remember that the bass triads we've been using are voiced 1–5–3. These voicings tend to work very well for making graceful harmonic modulations.

The most common inversion of a V chord triad places its 3rd in the bass, which also functions as a leading tone of the target chord, whose root is found a half step up. For example, G/B resolves to C. E/G# resolves to A. Here's the basic fingering for the first-inversion major chord in 1–5–1 based tunings.

You may recognize this voicing as the chord we're using for the iii and vii° chords in the diatonic bass triads. The chord we're using in place of the iii chord is actually I/3, a first-inversion I chord. In the key of D major, that's D/F# resolving to G (IV). So D, while obviously being the I chord, is heard briefly as the V of IV, largely because it has F# in the bass, acting as a leading tone to G.

In the following example this inversion allows us to ascend smoothly through the key of D major, alternating between the diatonic triads and their secondary dominants.

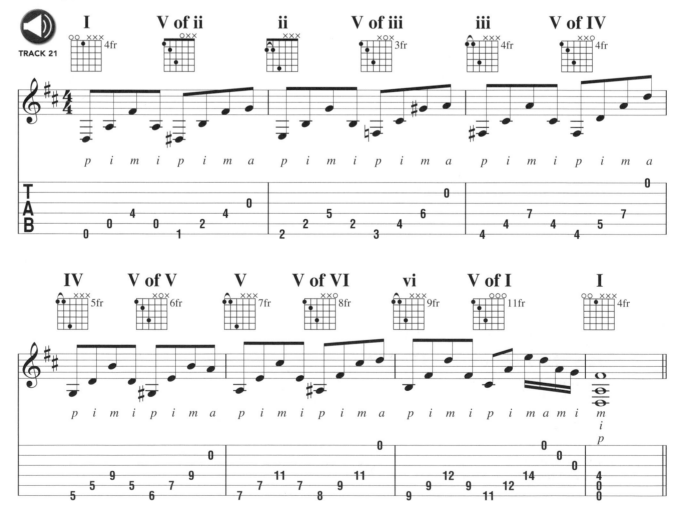

The 3–1–5 voiced triad inversion in the previous examples is one of four highly versatile voicings we'll examine next. In addition to various other ways they can function, these voicings can all function as V chords, each with multiple resolution points, depending on the surrounding chords. If each voicing has multiple resolution points, then, conversely, any point of resolution can be arrived at from multiple places.

To understand each chord's role as a V chord and its possible resolution points, we'll start by listening to how they resolve to I in the major key of the root string (D), but from various spots along the neck. This tends to make the implementation of these chords relatively easy since the key has been established by the preceding chords and strengthened by the open strings. In some cases the chord will be easily recognized on its own as a V chord, and in other cases it may need to be preceded by a ii, IV, or vi to function as such.

Keep in mind that if a chord can resolve to I, it can generally resolve to the relative minor (vi) as well, and sometimes to iii.

In the figure below, any chord on the left can be used to resolve to any chord on the right. On the left are the V shapes, followed by the frets from which they can resolve to the I or vi chord, as indicated. The chords' names and numbers are intentionally left off because they depend on where you play the chord relative to the tonic. On the right are some examples for I and vi.

In most cases, depending on the tuning, various open strings can be added for richness when complementary to the progression. As always, use your ears.

Context is everything in terms of where you can resolve a chord. To clearly define these chords in the role of V, try placing them between ii and I, to create a ii–V–I. Alternately you can use IV in place of ii, and vi in place of I, as mentioned.

A graceful resolution is largely dependent upon smooth voice leading in the upper notes of the chords. The next page

V	resolves from fret	to:	I or vi
V	2nd 5th 8th 11th	→	I (4fr)
V	2nd 5th 8th 11th	→	I (9fr)
V	1st 3rd 4th 5th 7th 8th 10th 11th	→	vi
V	1st 4th 7th 10th	→	vi (9fr)

contains three examples. Create at least six of your own resolutions, adding open strings where they complement the progression. Pay particular attention to the interval distance between the V chord and the tonic so you'll be able to easily apply it in other keys.

Tuning:
(low to high) D-A-D-G-A-D

Tuning:
(low to high) D-A-D-G-A-D

Tuning:
(low to high) D-A-D-G-A-D

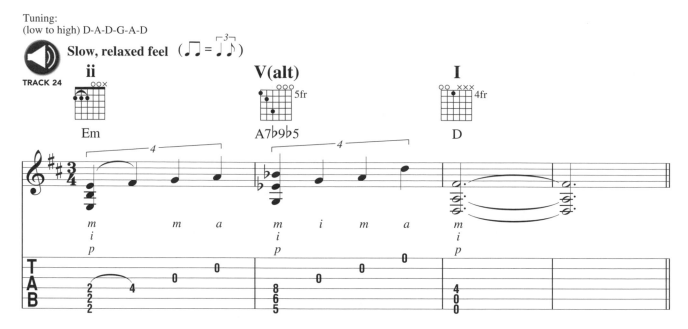

Longer Modulations and "The Loneliest Monk"

To observe some longer modulations in action, listen to this piece of mine called "The Loneliest Monk." It's in DADGAD but centers around a G tonic. You'll recognize many of the chords and see how they can be used in creating modulation.

Tuning:
(low to high) D-A-D-G-A-D

The Loneliest Monk

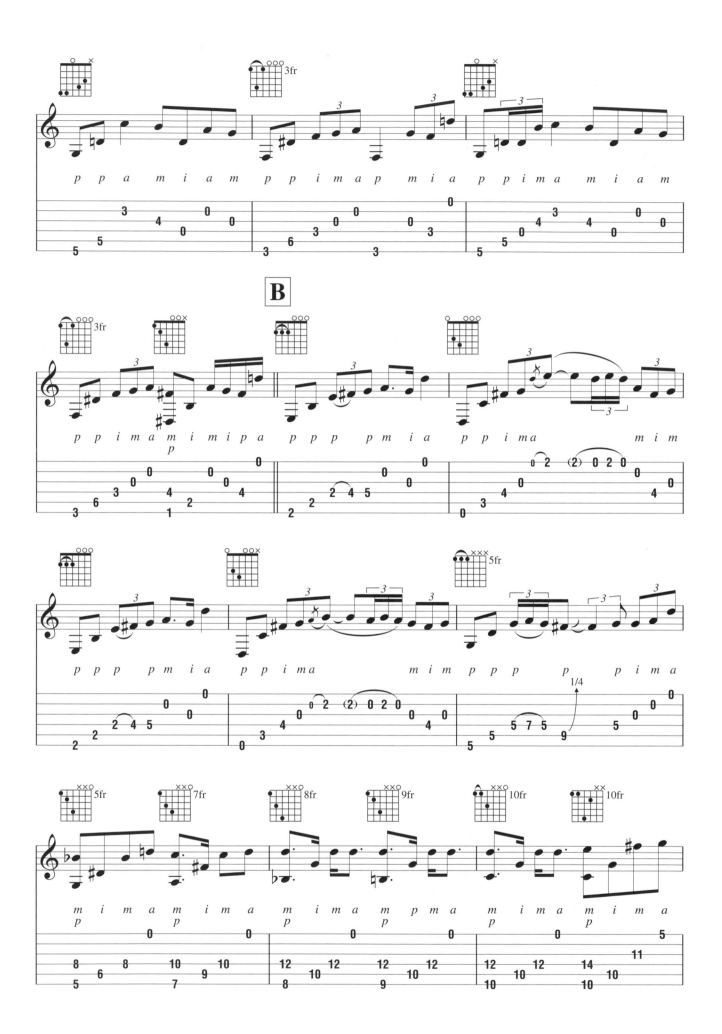

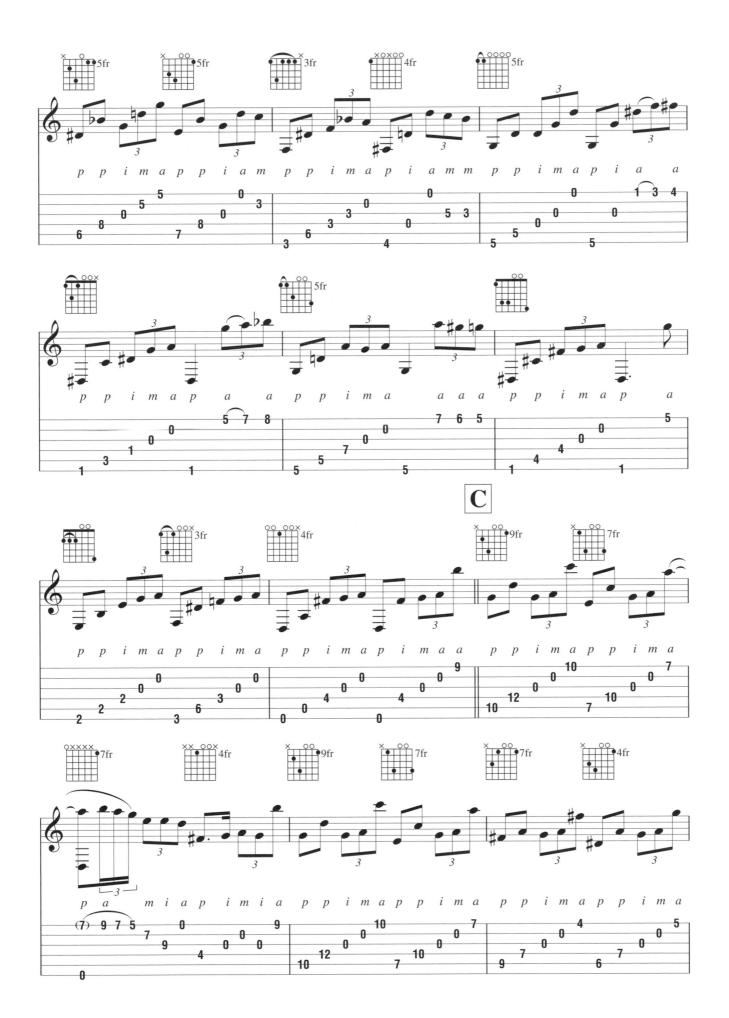

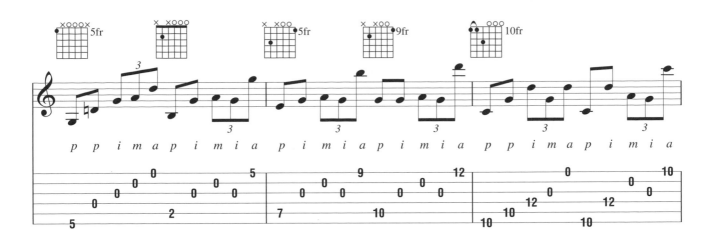

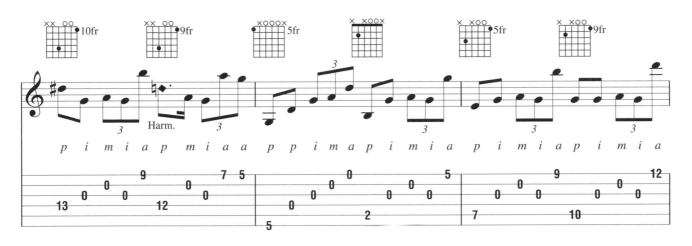

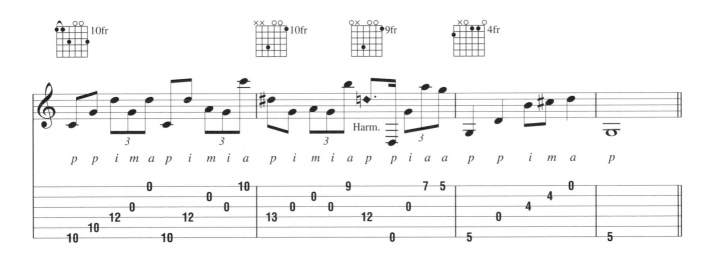

14

Non-Diatonic Scales, Chords, and Modes

So far throughout the book everything we've done has been in the diatonic realm. Even the pentatonic scale is comprised of notes from the diatonic scale.

In this chapter we'll look at three scales that fall outside diatonic harmony.

Harmonic Minor

The harmonic minor scale is the same as a natural minor scale but with a raised 7th. This note reflects the tonality of the major 3rd in the V chord of the minor tonic chord, e.g., E7 to Am. The major 3rd (G♯) in the E chord is the one note that falls outside of the diatonic key of A minor, and what gives this scale its defining edge.

You can use the harmonic minor scale over any minor or suspended tuning that doesn't contain a flat 7th, and even then it often works if the raised 7th is used in passing.

We'll use DADGAD, as its open strings harmonize quite well with the scale. Here are the bass triads with strict use of the harmonic minor notes. Play through them and learn them, including the open strings if you like. It's best to play them arpeggiated, instead of as block chords.

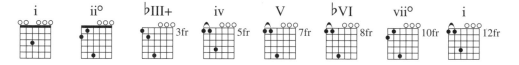

Here's another version with a variation in the way the middle voice ascends.

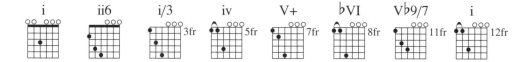

Here's a third version that's a hybrid between the harmonic minor and the natural minor. Any of the chords from these three sets can be freely mixed and matched.

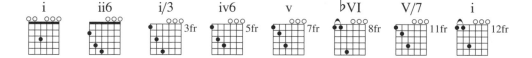

Spend some time getting these shapes under your fingers and using them to create chord progressions.

Melodic Minor

The melodic minor scale is basically a Dorian mode with a raised 7th. You could also look at it as a major scale with a flat 3rd, but it's better to see it as a variation of Dorian since it is a minor scale. We'll use the "jazz'" version of the melodic minor scale, wherein the notes of the scale are the same in both ascending and descending versions. In classical theory the scale reverts to natural minor when descending.

The chord shapes below work well over DADGAD, as well as over many other minor or suspended-type tunings. In each of the voicings, I have included a variation in the middle voice.

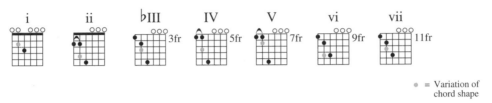

● = Variation of chord shape

Spanish Phrygian

The Spanish Phrygian scale, sometimes called called Phrygian Dominant, is the fifth mode of the harmonic minor scale. It is used extensively in flamenco music as well as many other traditions. If you've gotten the harmonic minor chord shapes under your fingers, it's only a slight adjustment to shift their placement to create the Spanish Phrygian set.

This is the primary scale used in my composition "Sketchy in Spain" from *What Worlds They Bring*. Here are the bass triad shapes for this scale. Try them over DADGCD. In each of the voicings, I have included a variation in the middle voice. These chords are beautifully rich in this tuning, but will work in many other tunings, including DADGAD.

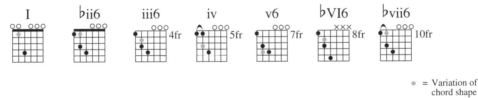

● = Variation of chord shape

Keep in mind that both the harmonic and melodic minor scales have seven modes, just like the diatonic scale. The possibilities are vast and fraught with strange and wondrous harmonies. Experiment with changing the tonic chord to create the various modes. This could keep you busy for several years if you really explore the harmonies.

These scales are just the tip of the non-diatonic iceberg. Be aware that these, as well as many other diatonic and non-diatonic scales, are often referred to by other names, depending on the culture or musical tradition.

I encourage you to expose your ears to as much music as you can from other cultures, and learn from that which inspires you.

SECTION FIVE: TECHNIQUES

15

Right-Hand Fingerstyle Technique

Good right-hand fingerstyle technique depends upon three primary factors: timing, overall tone, and consistency of volume and tone between each finger and the thumb. Underlying all these factors is the single most important thing to remember: **stay relaxed**. There is very little in life for which this is not good advice, but it's particularly important when doing something requiring the delicate finesse needed by the right hand in fingerstyle playing.

It's generally best, ergonomically speaking, to sit classical style with the left foot on a foot stool, or using a strap, so that the guitar hangs about where it would if you were using a foot stool. If you perform standing up as I do, it's a good idea to spend at least some of your practice time standing. Otherwise, you may find that you're not able to execute things as well on the gig as you could in your practice sessions.

Your right hand should hang comfortably in position, slightly angled, allowing the muscles to move in fluid motion.

If you feel like you're forcing it, pause, relax, and slow it down. As you practice an exercise or a piece, try playing it a little slower than you are capable, and see just how relaxed you can stay throughout. Make relaxation your primary concern. You'll sound much better and have more fun playing.

I use a thumbpick most of the time when fingerpicking, but it's a matter of personal taste and the style of music you're playing as to whether you should.

For open-tuning fingerstyle playing, I like the clarity I get from a thumbpick, whereas for fingerstyle jazz and Brazilian playing I prefer the roundness I get from the naked thumb.

It's important to keep in mind that, in addition to the various factors covered in this chapter, the state of your nails can dramatically affect every aspect of right-hand fingerstyle technique. See Chapter 20, "Nail Care," for detailed information.

16

Picking Patterns and Excerpts

Picking patterns play a major role in developing a musical vocabulary in fingerstyle playing. They not only define the rhythm but often will spawn a melodic idea that can be crafted into a well-defined melody.

Any pattern, regardless of how interesting it may be, can quickly start sounding stiff if repeated too many times without variation. Often, however, changing just one note within the pattern can keep it from sounding too repetitious.

The idea is to develop a widely-varied palette of patterns upon which you can draw spontaneously and creatively.

The patterns in the first section are demonstrated using various chords, progressions, and tunings that bring out that pattern's unique qualities. You'll find the right-hand fingerings below the notation. Start by playing the pattern over the open strings, adding the left hand only when you are comfortable with the right hand alone.

After getting a pattern under your fingers as written, spend some time playing it over some other chords or tunings until it becomes comfortable over any chord or progression you choose.

Any of the patterns will work over almost any chord. Find ways to integrate them and make them your own. Change the treble strings around if necessary to accommodate a particular chord or melody. The basic rhythmic groove is generally established on the bass strings so you can usually get away with changing around the treble strings while maintaining a solid rhythmic base.

Remember to play the examples *sostenuto*, letting the notes ring as long as possible. Listen to the examples to get the feel and accents right.

Tuning:
(low to high) D-A-D-G-C-D

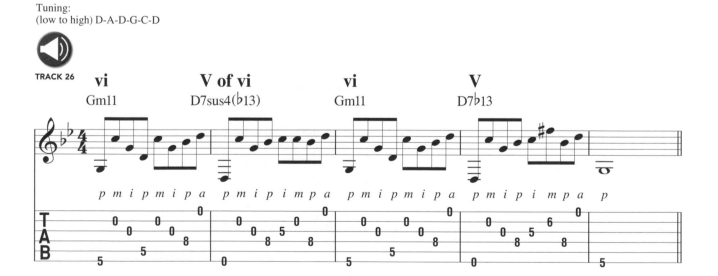

Tuning:
(low to high) E-B-E-G-A-D

TRACK 27

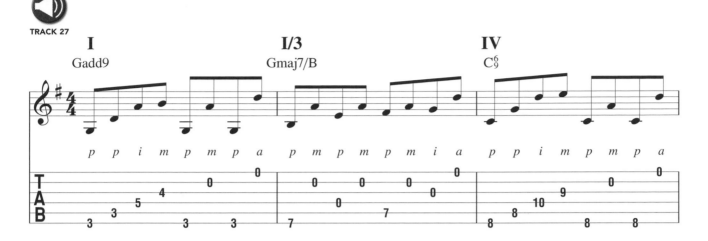

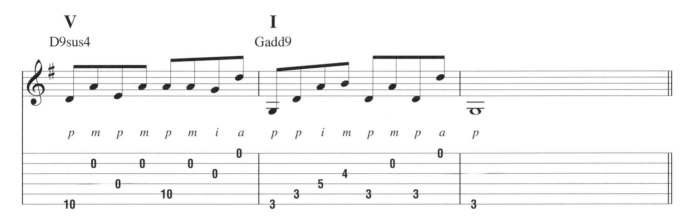

Capo II

Tuning:
(low to high) E-B-E-F#-A-B

TRACK 28

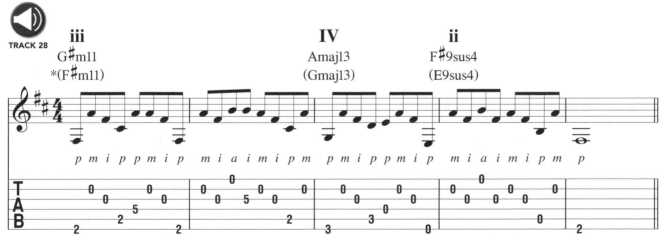

*Symbols in parentheses represent chord names respective to capoed guitar. Symbols above reflect actual sounding chords. Capoed fret is "0" in tab.

Capo II

Tuning:
(low to high) E-B-E-F♯-A-B

*Symbols in parentheses represent chord names respective to capoed guitar. Symbols above reflect actual sounding chords. Capoed fret is "0" in tab.

Capo II

Tuning:
(low to high) E-B-E-F♯-A-B

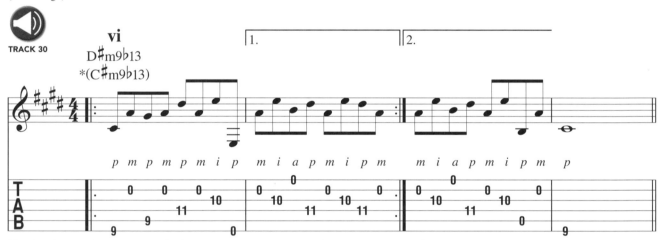

*Symbols in parentheses represent chord names respective to capoed guitar. Symbols above reflect actual sounding chords. Capoed fret is "0" in tab.

Tuning:
(low to high) E-B-E-G-A-D

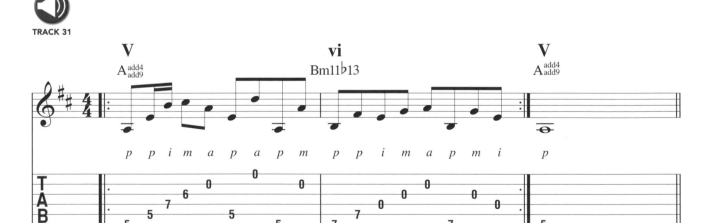

Tuning:
(low to high) E-B-E-F#-A-B

TRACK 32

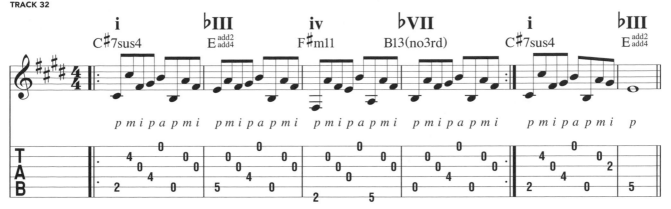

Capo II

Tuning:
(low to high) E-B-E-F#-A-B

TRACK 33

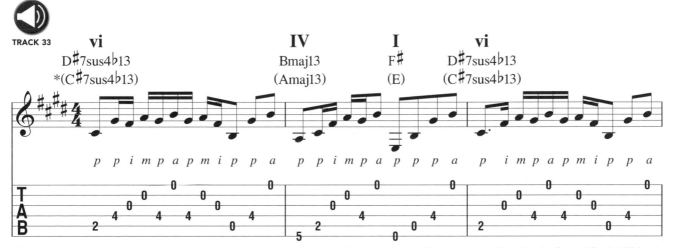

*Symbols in parentheses represent chord names respective to capoed guitar. Symbols above reflect actual sounding chords. Capoed fret is "0" in tab.

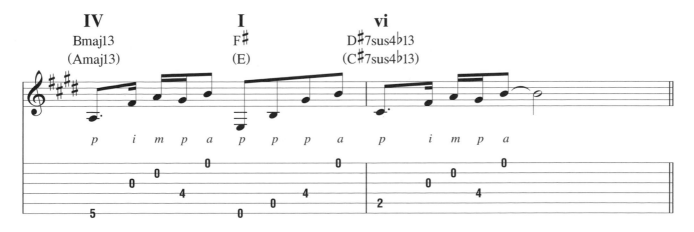

This example is based on a triplet feel and uses a hammer-on as part of the pattern. It will also work over just about any other chord where a note in the chord on the 4th or 5th string is hammerable.

Tuning:
(low to high) E-B-E-G-A-D

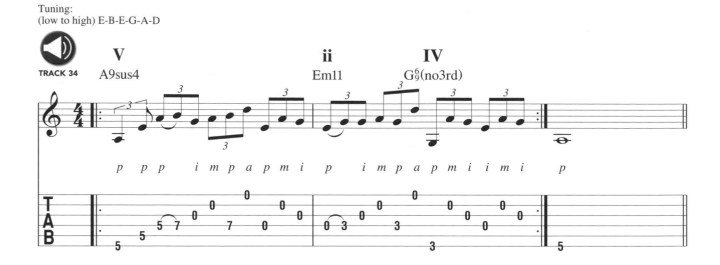

Patterns from Pieces

The following pattern examples are excerpted from pieces on CDs I've released.

This intro pattern, as well as most of "Sketchy in Spain" (from *What Worlds They Bring*), has a six-against-four feel. It can be felt either in 4/4, with the picking pattern felt as triplets, or in 6/8, with the picking pattern being felt as 8th notes. It is written here in 4/4 using triplets. The scale used here is Spanish Phrygian (see page 61 in Chaper 14, "Non-Diatonic Scales, Chords, and Modes").

Sketchy in Spain
INTRO

Tuning:
(low to high) D-A-D-G-C-D

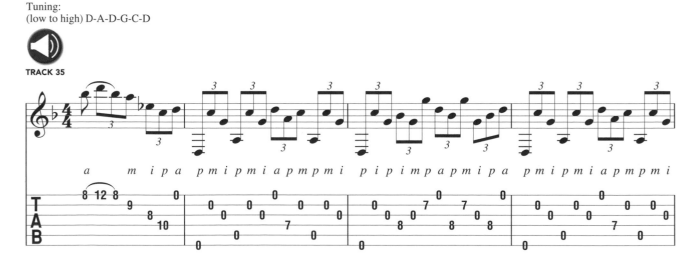

The next pattern is in 6/4. The driving force of this groove happens primarily on the 3rd and 4th unison strings, and is heavily dependent on the way they are accented. Be sure to listen to the recording to get it right. The pattern is written twice just to show that as it starts over it does not employ the "pinch," as in the very first measure. The recording fades out as the pattern goes into the next measure.

Open Story

Capo II

Tuning:
(low to high) D-A-E-E-B-F#

TRACK 36

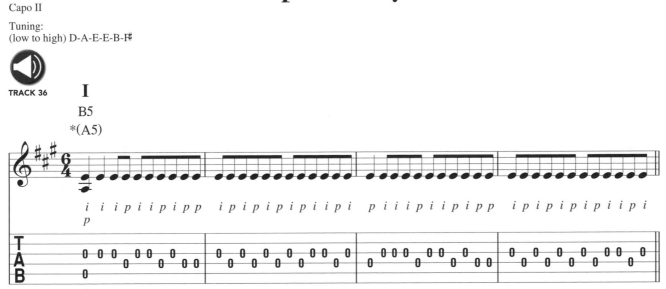

*Symbols in parentheses represent chord names respective to capoed guitar. Symbols above reflect actual sounding chords. Capoed fret is "0" in tab.

The next pattern is in 4/4 and built for speed, employing a couple of key hammer-ons in each measure. The hammer-ons combine with the fingerpicked notes to create a rapid-fire pattern. Good left-hand position, generally facilitated by either sitting classical style or standing using a strap, is essential for getting crisp hammer-ons that will stand up next to the fingerpicked notes.

Crescent

Capo II

Tuning:
(low to high) E-B-E-F#-B-D#

TRACK 37

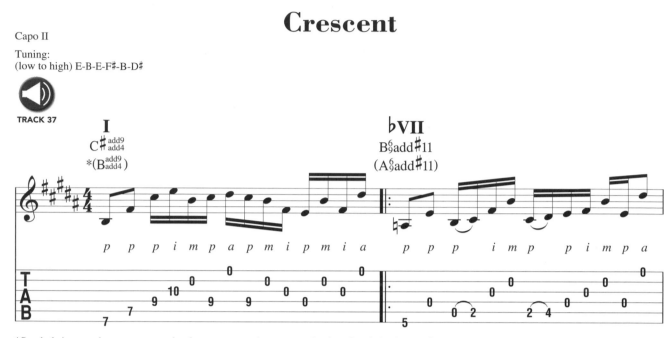

*Symbols in parentheses represent chord names respective to capoed guitar. Symbols above reflect actual sounding chords. Capoed fret is "0" in tab.

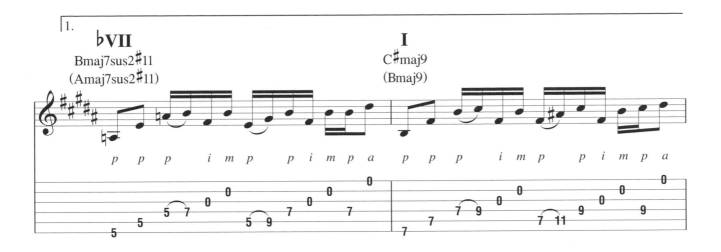

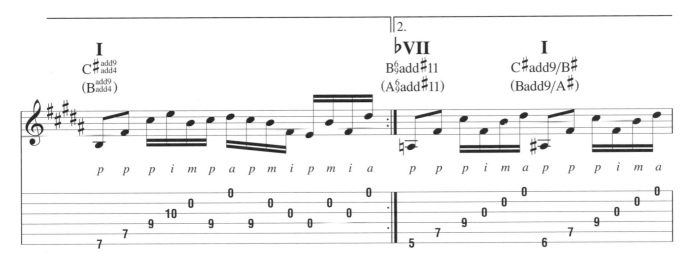

Creating Melody for Solo Guitar

In order to best understand the process of creating melody for solo guitar, let's look first at the idea of creating melody in general and break it into three groups.

1. The melody you're creating is what you're hearing in your head.

   It's that simple. You're purely creating melody. Maybe you're using your voice to bring to life what you're hearing in your head. Maybe you're an accomplished improviser, playing what you hear as a solo over chords.

2. The melody you're creating is what you're hearing, but altered where necessary to meet mechanical challenges. This includes any number of things, such as holding down a bassline, chords, and melody all at once.

3. The melody you're creating consists of phrases arising out of a pattern or facilitated by a tuning or specific technique, then refined to your liking.

Your voice, regardless of whether you are a good singer, is the most direct conduit to the melodies living inside you. If you haven't already, start using your voice to bring out the melodies you're hearing in your head.

My own compositions tend to be split about 50-50 between writing melody for two or more instruments and solo guitar writing. I find that the process of writing for solo guitar is vastly different as a result of the necessary consideration one needs to give to the mechanics of executing multiple parts in a solo context.

A melody that is completely voice-driven, while possibly brilliant, may or may not be practical for playing solo. Just because you *can* do it doesn't necessarily mean you should. It may need to be simplified so that you can hold down the necessary parts and still make it groove. Does it feel good to play?

I have my best results when there's an active give and take in the compositional process, frequently switching between the melody leading the way and the chords leading the way. Generally for me, in a solo context, compositions are much more chord-driven, with the melody being added later.

When composing melody for solo guitar, there are infinite possible melodies waiting to be discovered over any given chord progression. Find the ones that come naturally based on the voicings and range of your chords.

Try using fingers that are not occupied to fret notes that are reachable from the chord you're on. Often one new note thrown into the high end of a picking pattern can combine with the other notes in the pattern in surprising ways, causing a melody to leap out of the arpeggio. Other times it's more subtle, sparking a melodic idea that you can develop into a complete melody.

Deepen Your Vocabulary

One of the most important aspects of developing your ability to create melody is to deepen your melodic and harmonic vocabulary within a chosen idiom. For example, to be a good jazz player it's important not only to develop a solid understanding of jazz harmony, but also to learn lots of jazz melodies and licks from jazz solos. They become grist for the mill in your own creative endeavors, and are crucial in defining the style.

The same can be said of rock or country or Indian classical music. Think about it like this: A traditional Japanese melody played on a guitar and a blues guitar solo, while both comprised of notes from the pentatonic scale, are about as likely to get mistaken for one another as Tom Waits for Pavarotti.

In developing your creative voice and technical skill as a solo guitarist it's particularly important to listen to and learn solo pieces. Learn from those who've mastered the unique challenges of playing solo guitar.

Focus on learning solo pieces and melodic phrases in the style in which you want to improve. Where to start? Which pieces, which licks? The answer is simple: learn the ones you like. This is the music you resonate with, and will have the greatest success incorporating into your own creative lexicon.

Soloing in Tunings*

Why, when it takes half a lifetime to solo well in standard tuning, would you want to try to master soloing in an alternate tuning? The answer is that you probably wouldn't try to master it, but rather to use it either when the tuning provides some unique sound or fingering that can't be achieved in standard tuning, or by necessity in a live situation.

Maybe the melody or some cool tapping thing needs to be played in an alternate tuning but you also want to take a single-note-type solo over the chords. There often is simply not enough time to make a guitar change, especially if you have to switch back to play the "cool part" on the other guitar.

There are basically two ways you could approach soloing in a tuning, with every shade of gray in between. They reflect the first and third situations I talked about in the beginning of this chapter. One way is to play what you hear, and the other is to stick to fingerings you've practiced and are familiar with. More often than not, soloing even in standard tuning involves elements of both approaches.

Finding string relationships that mirror standard tuning is vital to soloing in any tuning.

*Single-note soloing in a duo or ensemble context

18

Tapping Technique

In this chapter, we'll be covering the basic fundamentals of tapping on acoustic guitar. I distinctly specify acoustic because it involves a completely different technique and approach from tapping on electric guitar. An electric guitar can be nearly as touch-sensitive as a touch instrument such as the Chapman Stick. This means there is no need to come down hard on the string for it to sound. This is both its strength and its weakness. While it allows for the complex piano-like independence between the hands, the sound of these instruments is generally lacking in dynamic range and attack. If a light touch produces relatively high volume, it leaves little room to get louder when you play harder.

Contrast that with acoustic tapping, wherein the velocity of attack needed to get a clear tone is such that only some notes and chords are possible in any given tuning. While you could set an acoustic guitar up with super-low action and light strings, it would defeat some of the main characteristics that give acoustic tapping its unique beauty, namely its rhythmic drive and chiming harmonics that come with a percussive attack.

I talked in the last chapter about the idea of playing what you hear, compared with playing on an instrument or in a tuning you don't entirely know, which is bound to surprise you. My approach to acoustic tapping often begins with the latter and is then driven by phrases and harmonies I hear and want to develop.

I approach the instrument almost like a drum with lots of notes on it. I start out tapping a rhythm on notes that make a good-sounding melodic pattern and let things develop from there, listening for a melody to emerge as I slowly begin to change the strings or frets in the pattern. When I hear something I like I try to develop it, without sacrificing the groove. The groove is the most important and should never be sacrificed in an attempt to incorporate melodies.

I've always enjoyed beating out rhythms on the nearest available surface, starting with the kitchen table. While this is a great way to hone your rhythmic sense, those around you may not find quite the same level of enjoyment in it as do you, thinking you resemble a nine-year-old overdosing on sugar. Fortunately there are ways to do it nearly silently on your own body. In any case, if you get the rhythm into your body by practicing on a table or your knees or whatever, it will go a long way towards helping you tap it out on the guitar.

Let's start by learning a basic 4/4 rhythm using a combination of tapping, hammer-ons, and pull-offs with both hands. Tap the string with some energy behind it, but in a very relaxed way, not unlike the action of cracking a whip. If your right-hand nails are getting in the way, just angle your hand back a little so that the nails clear the string. You don't have to tap with the very tip of the finger. Medium to low action works best, and a capo is imperative. A magnetic pickup will greatly enhance the sound of tapping (especially in the low end) by bringing more of the note and less of the metallic sound of the string hitting the fret.

All numbers adjacent to notes in the notation staff represent left-hand tapping fingers, which should be hammered down on the indicated frets—otherwise known as "hammering from nowhere." The left-hand tapping is also visually reinforced in the notation with half slurs. Right-hand taps are shown with a "+" symbol above the notation and a "T" above the tab staff. Right-hand tapping fingerings are also shown with the standard "*p-i-m-a*" symbols.

Capo II

Tuning:
(low to high) D-A-D-G-C-D

TRACK 38

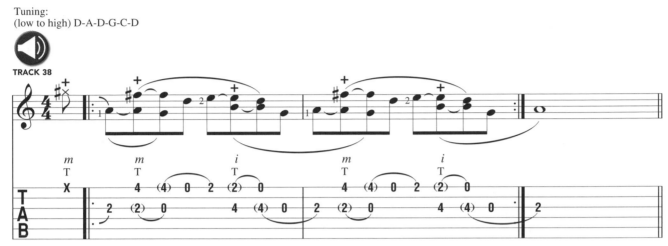

On the next page you'll find a transcription of "Rodeo Carousel." It is played entirely with tapping technique. The tapping notation used here is the same as in the Track 38 example. Consult the Key below for additional symbols and techniques used in this piece. Go slowly, learning and memorizing short segments before moving on.

"RODEO CAROUSEL"

KEY

TS = Thumb Slap (use outside knuckle of right thumb like slapping on electric bass)

SL = Slap strings with index finger of right hand

SL Harm. = Slap strings at 12th fret to produce harmonics

ST = Strum strings with a left-hand finger (downward across the fretboard)

Rodeo Carousel

Capo II

Open C tuning:
(low to high) C-G-C-G-C-E

Sostenuto

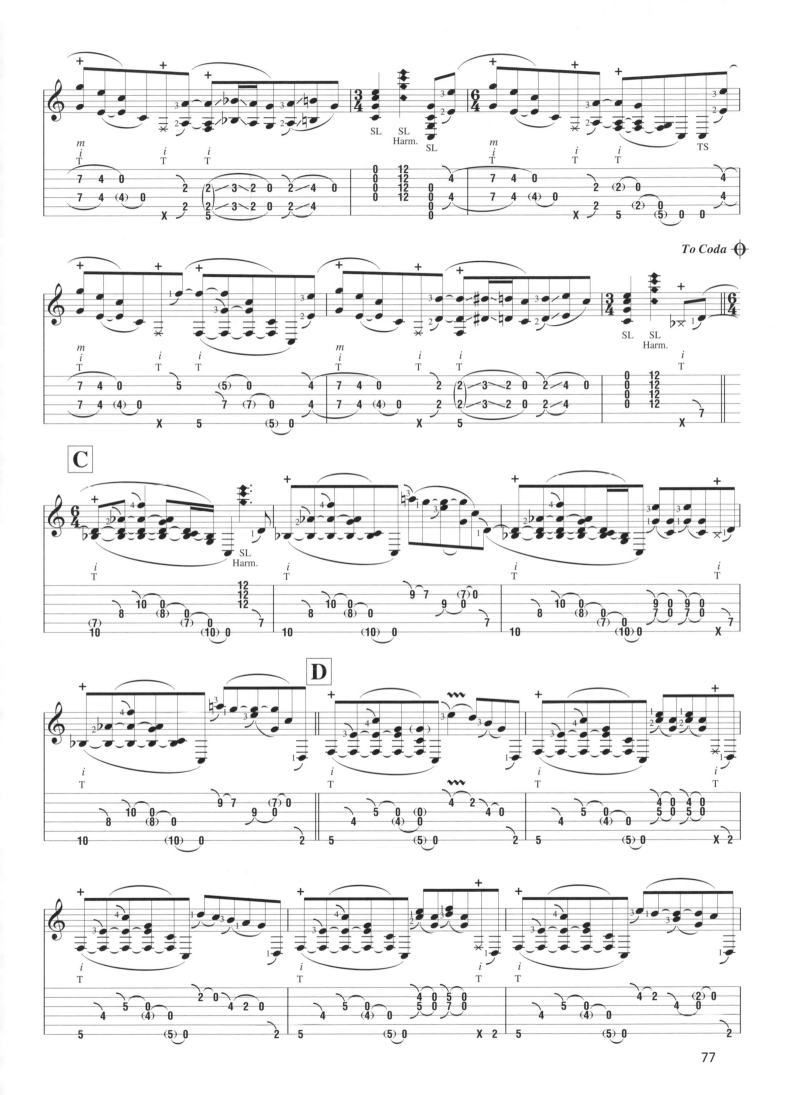

Coda

D.S. al Coda

E2

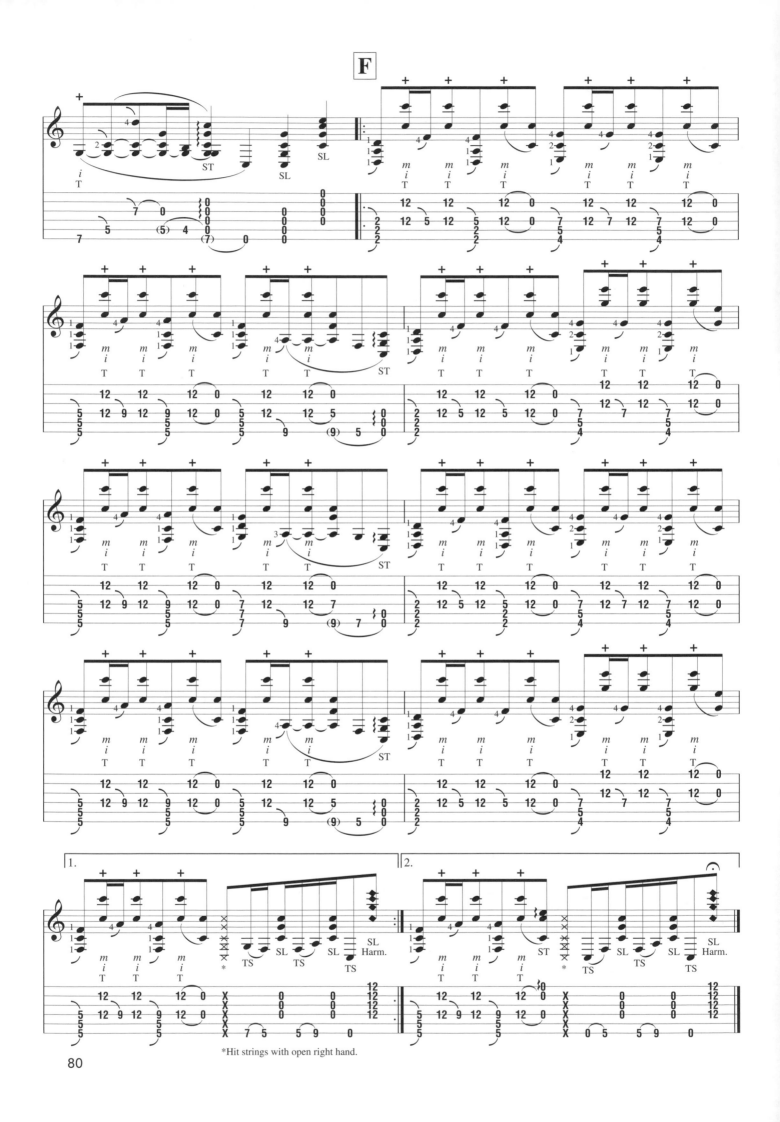

*Hit strings with open right hand.

19
Slap Technique

The technique demonstrated in this chapter is essentially slap funk bass technique adapted for guitar to incorporate strumming. The slap is created by hitting a low string with the side of the thumb knuckle. It's essential to keep your hand very relaxed so that the thumb can bounce off the string when you hit it. The power comes from a relaxed flicking approach, not from brute force. Sometimes you want the note to sound loud and clear, and other times you want a totally dead note for its percussive effect.

Slapping is usually used in conjunction with *popping*, a technique in which a finger is hooked under the string, pulling it away from the neck, so that it slaps back against the frets when released. For guitar the first finger usually works best for popping.

It is outside the scope of this book to cover slap funk bass technique in detail, but there are volumes written on the subject, along with countless DVDs and web sites. Suffice to say, if you need more explanation, there's no shortage.

In this example you'll find a combination of slap technique with traditional strumming. I usually use the nail of my first finger for the strummed parts. As you'll see in the example, the strums are written for specific strings. It is not a critical error, however, if you hit or miss a string not included in the group.

Tuning:
(low to high) Db-Ab-Db-Gb-B-Db

TRACK 40

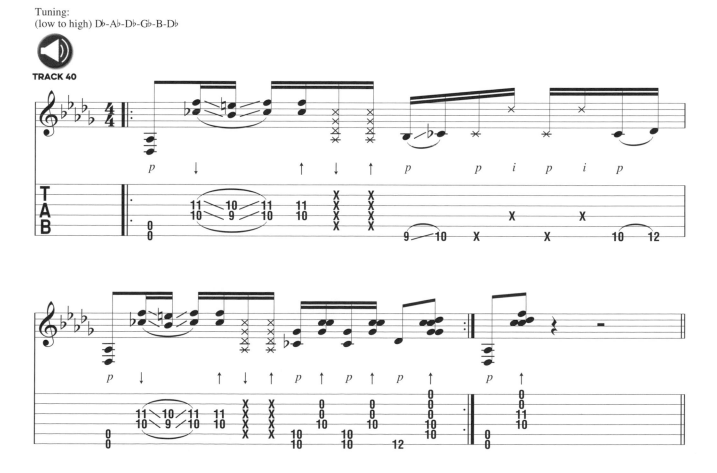

⑳
Essential Tips

Tuning Tips

For every tuning you use, you should have a tuning chord comprised solely of roots and 5ths to check the tuning. For this purpose, stay away from major chords. In our tempered system of tuning, the major 3rd is considerably sharp—and the minor 3rd slightly so—from the natural harmonics of the overtone series. As a result, it is impossible to get a major or a minor chord perfectly in tune without throwing off the tuning of other chords.

Here are some tuning chords for a few tunings:

| DADGAD | DADGCD | DADG♯AE | EBEF♯BE | EBEF♯AD | Standard | CGCGCE (Open C) |

Make sure you have your intonation adjusted by someone who knows what they are doing. It is difficult if not impossible to get a badly-intonated guitar in tune. As you start to get used to an out-of-tune guitar, there's a tendency to become less sensitive to pitch. Though not a permanent condition, it may make you less popular with the other boys and girls in music class.

Always do your fine tuning after the capo is on the desired fret. Keep in mind that it is not necessary to take the capo off when moving between tunings.

Always check your tuning if you move the capo, even if you are only adjusting its angle.

Always make sure your last turn of the peg comes from below the pitch. If the string is sharp, dip down slightly below the pitch and come back up. This is especially necessary when a capo is used, but is essential in all cases to maintain string tension on both sides of the capo or nut. Otherwise the string is likely to get pulled out of tune once you start playing.

TUNING IN PERFORMANCE

One of the biggest challenges of performing in alternate tunings is holding the audience's attention between tunes while getting in and out of various tunings. There are many ways of addressing this to maintain the show's momentum.

Here are some suggestions:

- Gather a few interesting stories to tell while tuning and practice telling them at home while you're tuning (no more than one story per tune or you risk public stoning).

- Order the songs so you don't have radical tuning changes early in the set.

- Tune as much as possible using the aforementioned tuning chords. You can make tuning a relatively pleasant thing to hear, or at least not as irritating as it can be if you tune the 3rd string to the 4th string and then the 2nd string to the 3rd, etc., constantly changing the tonal center the audience hears.

- Always have an electronic tuner on stage to fall back on in case you're having trouble hearing on stage.

- Have extra strings and a string winder on stage in case of breakage.

- Having multiple pre-tuned guitars on stage is another option.

- Hiring someone who is capable of tuning an alternate guitar (while you're playing) that can be switched out between songs is ideal, if you have the means.

String and Capo Tips

STRINGS

Try to keep new or fresh-sounding strings on your guitar. It can mean the difference between feeling inspired or hopelessly depressed, ready to quit music.

On acoustic guitar, I use medium gauge phosphor bronze strings. I like the brightness and timbre of the phosphor bronze, and prefer medium over light gauge for the increased volume and sustain. They are also better suited for certain tunings that include lower pitches, and tuning them up a half or whole step is generally fine. I regularly tune my 1st, 2nd, 4th, and 5th strings up a whole step and have never had a problem with breakage or tension on the neck or top.

As far as string breakage is concerned, I've found that it has much less to do with tuning up high and more to do with friction and/or metal fatigue. Every instrument has its idiosyncrasies, but with a bit of preparation, you can make breakage an extremely rare event.

Here are a couple of things you can do to avoid an untimely breakage:

- Pull the string to the side out of its slot in the nut, and using a regular wooden pencil, roll the lead around the nut slot to get some graphite in there. Then put the string back. This will lubricate the slot and cut down considerably on the friction that causes strings to break near the headstock. It also makes the nut last much longer by preventing the string from sawing its way deeper into the slot. If you've never had a new nut made, you may want to. A bone nut is best. Consult your local repair person.

- If you break strings near the bridge, check the saddle and make sure the edge of the saddle on which the string rests is not too sharp. Again, consult your local repair person. While you're at it, you might want to have your intonation checked, and if necessary, have a new saddle made. Always use a bone saddle.

CAPOS

There are many things on a stringed instrument that are only possible in tunings containing certain open-string relationships. If you're playing music that relies heavily upon the use of open strings or string relationships, you might want to use a capo to change the key while retaining the qualities of the open strings.

Having this flexibility may be necessary when playing with other people, especially with singers. For playing styles that do not rely on open strings, such as jazz and Brazilian music, a capo is not generally very useful; nor are alternate tunings, for that matter.

A capo lowers the guitar's action considerably, which may be necessary for certain techniques such as tapping. Also, there are some things that just sound better in certain keys, or with the somewhat brighter and tighter sound produced when using a capo.

I use a capo for all of my pieces where intricate tapping is involved, usually placed at the 2nd fret, and sometimes at the 4th. Besides the obvious loss of a few lower pitches, you also lose some low end frequencies due to a shorter string length. You'll get all of this low end back and then some with the use of a magnetic pickup. In a recording situation in which you are not using a pickup, you can usually get all the low end you need with careful mic placement, although for tapping I still include a magnetic pickup.

For anything that involves playing more than a few frets higher than the capoed fret, you might want to stay away from capoing at the 1st, 3rd, and even 5th fret, as it puts the fingerboard dots in the wrong places. Personally, I find this distracting. If you stick to the 2nd, 4th, or 6th fret, it will give you the first two or three dots correctly placed. If you are after a particular key, you can usually compensate by tuning up or down a half step to accommodate the desired capo placement. If you're capoing above the 6th fret, this is much less important as the frets are much closer together and the neck range shortened.

Some players cut slots in the capo to allow certain strings to remain un-capoed, and some manufacturers are even making capos now with the slots pre-cut. I haven't spent enough time with them to recommend them one way or the other, but some players swear by them.

Nail Care

The nails not only play a huge role in your tone, but also can affect your timing. The best length for a nail can vary from finger to finger or player to player. It's important that both flesh and nail make contact with the string and that all three fingers glide over the strings with a similar amount of resistance. Try to get a similar tone from each finger and each nail. You should think of your nails as part of your instrument. They often make a bigger difference in the sound than the guitar itself.

KEEP YOUR NAILS HEALTHY

Regardless of whether you use anything artificial on your nails, you want to keep the nail and nail bed as healthy as possible. Taking calcium and magnesium supplements can definitely help to build strong nails. Borage oil, evening primrose oil, and black currant oil taken internally are also widely reported to promote nail growth, as they are a natural source of gamma-linolenic acid (GLA). There is a myth that taking gelatin will make your nails strong. Gelatin has little or no effect on nail growth.

There are also many topical oils and creams that help the nails keep from getting brittle and may help them grow faster. It's best to choose a natural product, and definitely stay away from anything with formaldehyde in it.

NAIL FILES AND SANDPAPER

You should have a number of different files, from medium grit for the initial shaping to ultra fine (gray surface) for the final buffing. Most drugstores carry multi-surface files that include the gray surface and a couple of coarser ones. You can also use sandpaper, which is a lot cheaper. 600 grit or finer works well for the final buffing. If you're making an artificial nail reinforcement you'll need a very coarse file to start out.

REAL VS. REINFORCED OR ARTIFICIAL NAILS

If you are blessed with strong nails you may not need to resort to any kind of artificial nails. You may still use this method however, to repair a crack until your nail grows out. I prefer to use the full reinforcements for fingerpicking night after night on steel strings. If your nails are on the thin side, the reinforcements can improve your tone as well as keep the nails from getting broken or worn down.

I also use the first fingernail as a flatpick, for which you definitely need a reinforced nail. I gave up the flatpick years ago, finding that I could execute everything as well or better with the nail, and with much better tone. You need a fairly thick reinforcement for this.

Personally, I don't like the type of acrylic nails they do at a salon, mainly because the acrylic is very destructive to your real nails. Over the years, I've experimented with nearly everything out there—and some that are really out there—and I've settled on a slightly enhanced version of a method many players use to repair a crack in a nail. This method works well to simply reinforce your own nails and also to extend the length until your own nail grows out.

MAKING A REINFORCED NAIL

You'll need:
- Regular or thin cyanoacrylate (such as Krazy Glue)
- Kleenex tissues
- Cyanoacrylate accelerator* if you're in a hurry
- It's not a bad idea also to have some cyanoacrylate debonder, also sold as Krazy Glue remover, in case you spill. Most model shops and some hardware stores carry accelerator and debonder. I prefer to use a non-whitening accelerator. The regular kind makes the glue turn bright white.
- Isopropyl (rubbing) alcohol

*Reinforcements enhanced with an accelerator will not last quite as long as those allowed to dry naturally.

MAKING A REINFORCED NAIL (cont.)

1. Start by cleaning the nail with isopropyl alcohol.

2. Take a piece of the tissue and separate its two plies.

3. Cut a small piece that covers the width of the nail to be treated. The length should be about the same or a little shorter than the nail. It should be placed so as to cover about half the length of the nail, with an ⅛" or more extending out over the end.

NOTE: If you want to extend the length of your own nail, you can leave a little more sticking out, so that once it dries and it is filed to the proper contour, there's still enough length. I don't recommend trying to extend your nail much more than 1/8" after it's filed down using this method. It's possible but pretty tricky.

4. Next put a drop or two of glue onto the nail and tissue (enough to saturate the tissue and no more). If the tissue goes onto the nail off center you can quickly move it back with the tip of the glue bottle before the glue sets. If you can't move it to where you want it in time, wipe it off, file off any excess glue or tissue and start over.

5. Let this layer dry for about three minutes. It's better not to use accelerator on this first layer. If you're trying to extend the length, wait until it's completely dry, about ten minutes or so. The portion of the tissue extending over the nail needs to be stable enough to act as a shell on which additional layers are added.

6. Take another piece of tissue and cut up a few more pieces around the same size. (Don't separate the plies this time.)

7. Now you can add more layers until you have the thickness you want; anywhere from three to eight is good. Wait about a minute between adding layers. Make sure that as you're adding layers, they are flush against the previous layer. You can use the tip of the glue bottle to smooth any air bubbles or separations as you go.

8. Let this dry completely. (If you can still smell the glue, it's not dry.) If you're using accelerator, spray a little on now but make it the smallest amount possible. A tiny bit will make it dry instantly. Too much will make your nail uncomfortably hot for thirty seconds or so.

9. Start with a coarse nail file and file it down until you have more or less the shape you want. Then using a medium file, fine-tune the shape and thickness. End by buffing it with a fine nail file, or 600-grit or finer sandpaper, until it's very smooth.

The reinforcements generally stay on for three weeks or so; however they do sometimes start to separate from the nail a little bit along the inside edge. At the first sign of this happening, you should glue it back down. If necessary, you can push down slightly on the opposite side of the reinforcement from where it's coming up so as to raise the edge. Then put a drop of glue under the reinforcement and push it back down.

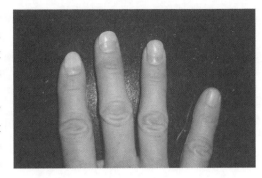

When the reinforcement does come off, you should coat the nail with tea tree oil, and from time to time it's not a bad idea to let it breathe for anywhere from an hour to overnight. Tea tree oil is a natural disinfectant and anti-fungal agent and can be purchased at any health food store.

Learning and the Muse

The general focus of this book has been to equip you with the theory, fingerboard knowledge, and technique to help you play creatively in alternate tunings. To this end I just want to remind you of the importance of taking time to learn music that inspires you. This is a very important aspect of becoming a good musician and can fuel the creative fire of even the most seasoned player.

The world's best composers and improvisers have generally spent a lot of time learning tunes, studying composition, copping licks, etc. Whenever I finish an album, I make a point of going into learning mode. This is a time when I shift my focus from output to input. It may be learning a classical piece or an Indian raga or a Russian folk melody; whatever inspires me at the time.

The creative muse is notoriously elusive and cannot be forced. My final words of advice: when you're feeling creative, create; when you're not, learn something.

Chord Construction

This page explains the construction of chords. Learn a little at a time until you know it all.

Triads:

Major	1	3	5
Minor	1	♭3	5
Diminished	1	♭3	♭5
Augmented	1	3	♯5

Though not officially triads, these two chord types are best grouped along with them.

*sus2	1	2	5
sus4	1	4	5

Seventh Chords:

Major 7th	1	3	5	7
Dominant 7th	1	3	5	♭7
Minor 7th	1	♭3	5	♭7
Minor 7th (♭5)	1	♭3	♭5	♭7
7sus4	1	4	5	♭7
Augmented 7th	1	3	♯5	♭7
Diminished 7th	1	♭3	♭5	♭♭7**

6th Chords:

6th	1	3	5	6
Minor 6th	1	♭3	5	6
Suspended 6th	1	4	5	6

9th Chords:

Formed by adding a 9th to any type of seventh chord. The chord name will remain the same except that "9" is used in place of "7," e.g., major 7 becomes major 9, minor 7 becomes minor 9, etc. (Note: The 9th is the same note as the 2nd.)

Add 9 Chords:

Formed by adding a 9th to any type of triad. They are written either using the word "add" (preferred) or abbreviated using only the 9, but in parentheses, i.e., Cadd9 or C(9). (Note: These differ from 9th chords in that the 7th is not included in add9 chords.)

*Also written as "2," e.g., D2.

**The ♭♭7 is enharmonic with the 6th.

13th Chords:

Formed by adding a 13th to any type of seventh chord. The chord name will remain the same except that "13" is used in place of "7," e.g., major 7 becomes major 13, minor 7 becomes minor 13, etc. (Note: The 13th is the same note as the 6th. They differ from 6th chords in that the 7th is present in 13th chords.)

11th Chords:

Formed by adding an 11th to any type of seventh chord. The chord name will remain the same except that "11" is used in place of "7," i.e., major 7 becomes major 11, minor 7 becomes minor 11, etc. (Note: The 11th is the same note as the 4th. 11th chords differ from suspended chords in that the 3rd is present in 11th chords.)

Add 4 Chords:

Formed by adding a 4th (or an 11th) to any type of triad. They are either written using the word "add," or abbreviated using only the 4, but in parentheses, e.g., Cadd4 (preferred) or C(4). Sometimes "add11" is used. (Note: This chord differs from 11th chords in that the 7th is not included in add4 chords.)

♯'s and ♭'s:

Any degree of a chord can be raised or lowered by a half step by simply placing ♯ or ♭ before the degree, e.g., C7♯5 is formed like this: 1 3 ♯5 ♭7

Slash (/) Chords:

Any chord can be followed by a "/" and a note indicating a different bass note, e.g., C/E is a C major triad with E in the bass.

Symbols:

- △ Major, but always followed by a number (e.g., C△7 or C△13).
- - Minor, usually followed by a number (e.g., C-6).
- ° Diminished (e.g., C° or C°7).
- ø Half diminished or m7♭5 (e.g., Cø)

Major Scale Formula

```
I   ii   iii   IV   V   vi   vii   I
 \/   \/   \/    \/   \/   \/    \/
 W    W    h    W    W    W    h
```

W: whole step
h: half step

Diatonic Triads in All Keys

C Major
I   C
ii   Dm
iii   Em
IV   F
V   G
vi   Am
vii   B°

G Major
I   G
ii   Am
iii   Bm
IV   C
V   D
vi   Em
vii   F♯°

D Major
I   D
ii   Em
iii   F♯m
IV   G
V   A
vi   Bm
vii   C♯°

A Major
I   A
ii   Bm
iii   C♯m
IV   D
V   E
vi   F♯m
vii   G♯°

E Major
I   E
ii   F♯m
iii   G♯m
IV   A
V   B
vi   C♯m
vii   D♯°

B Major
I   B
ii   C♯m
iii   D♯m
IV   E
V   F♯
vi   G♯m
vii   A♯°

F Major
I   F
ii   Gm
iii   Am
IV   B♭
V   C
vi   Dm
vii   E°

B♭ Major
I   B♭
ii   Cm
iii   Dm
IV   E♭
V   F
vi   Gm
vii   A°

E♭ Major
I   E♭
ii   Fm
iii   Gm
IV   A♭
V   B♭
vi   Cm
vii   D°

A♭ Major
I   A♭
ii   B♭m
iii   Cm
IV   D♭
V   E♭
vi   Fm
vii   G°

D♭ Major
I   D♭
ii   E♭m
iii   Fm
IV   G♭
V   A♭
vi   B♭m
vii   C°

G♭ Major
I   G♭
ii   A♭m
iii   B♭m
IV   C♭
V   D♭
vi   E♭m
vii   F°

Diatonic Seventh Chords in All Keys

C Major
I   Cmaj7
ii   Dm7
iii   Em7
IV   Fmaj7
V   G7
vi   Am7
vii   Bm7♭5

E Major
I   Emaj7
ii   F♯m7
iii   G♯m7
IV   Amaj7
V   B7
vi   C♯m7
vii   Dm7♭5

E♭ Major
I   E♭maj7
ii   Fm7
iii   Gm7
IV   A♭maj7
V   B♭7
vi   Cm7
vii   Dm7♭5

G Major
I   Gmaj7
ii   Am7
iii   Bm7
IV   Cmaj7
V   D7
vi   Em7
vii   F♯m7♭5

B Major
I   Bmaj7
ii   C♯m7
iii   D♯m7
IV   Emaj7
V   F♯7
vi   G♯m7
vii   Am7♭5

A♭ Major
I   A♭maj7
ii   B♭m7
iii   Cm7
IV   D♭maj7
V   E♭7
vi   Fm7
vii   Gm7♭5

D Major
I   Dmaj7
ii   Em7
iii   F♯m7
IV   Gmaj7
V   A7
vi   Bm7
vii   Cm7♭5

F Major
I   Fmaj7
ii   Gm7
iii   Am7
IV   B♭maj7
V   C7
vi   Dm7
vii   Em7♭5

D♭ Major
I   D♭maj7
ii   E♭m7
iii   Fm7
IV   G♭maj7
V   A♭7
vi   B♭m7
vii   Cm7♭5

A Major
I   Amaj7
ii   Bm7
iii   C♯m7
IV   Dmaj7
V   E7
vi   F♯m7
vii   Gm7♭5

B♭ Major
I   B♭maj7
ii   Cm7
iii   Dm7
IV   E♭maj7
V   F7
vi   Gm7
vii   Am7♭5

G♭ Major
I   G♭maj7
ii   A♭m7
iii   B♭m7
IV   C♭maj7
V   D♭7
vi   E♭m7
vii   Fm7♭5

Extended Diatonic Chord Functions

There are many chords besides maj7, m7, dominant 7th, and m7♭5 that can also function as one of the seven diatonic chords. Some are just extensions of the basic 1–3–5–7 voicings, and some are quite different. Below is a chart of such chords and how they can function. Where there is more than one possible function listed, the other chords in the progression and/or the melody need to be considered.

CHORD	FUNCTION*
maj9 or maj13	I or IV
maj11	I
9, 11, or 13	V
m9	ii or vi
m11	ii, iii, or vi
m6 or m13	ii
6th	I or IV
sus4	I, ii, iii, V, or VI
7sus4	ii, iii, vi, or V
9sus4	V, ii, or vi
13sus4	V or ii
add9, (9)	I or IV
add4 or add11, (4 or 11)	I
m(add9)	ii or vi
m7♯5	iii or vii
sus2 (also written as "2," e.g., D2)	I, ii, IV, V, or vi

*It should be noted that just because a function is listed for a chord doesn't necessarily mean it can be used as a chord substitution for the 1–3–5–7 version. It just means that the diatonic mode of the same number may work over it.

Diatonic Bass Triads for 1–5–1 Tunings

The Locrian mode was omitted because it is very unstable and rarely acts as a tonic.

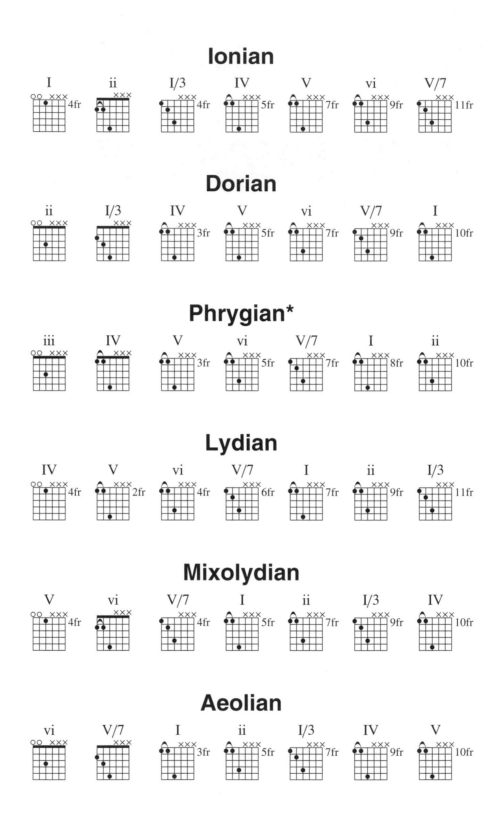

*Notice in Phrygian I/3 is not used in place of the III chord as in all the other modes. This is because it is the tonic and the I/3 chord is not a resolved chord, and thus is used most commonly in transition.

Extended Bass Chords for 1-5-1 Tunings

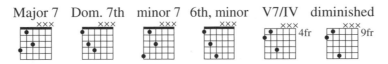

Major 7   Dom. 7th   minor 7   6th, minor   V7/IV   diminished

Danny Heines Tunings List
(NC = No Capo)

TUNING	PIECES	CAPO FRET	ALBUM
D A D G A D 1 5 1 4 5 1	The Loneliest Monk Six Picture Dream Burning Angel	NC NC 4	*What Worlds They Bring* *What Worlds They Bring* *Vanishing Borders*
D A D G C D 1 5 1 4 ♭7 1	Sketchy in Spain	NC	*What Worlds They Bring*
D A D G C D (Hi-Strung)	Piercing With	NC	*Vanishing Borders*
D A D G♯ A E 1 5 1 ♯4 5 9	Faster Than Alone	NC	*Vanishing Borders*
D A E E B F♯ 1 5 9 9 6 3	Open Story	2	*Every Island*
D A E F♯ A E 1 5 9 3 5 9	September Snow	2	*Aqua Touch*
D A D G C D 1 5 1 4 ♭7 1	Boy on a Zebra	NC	*Vanishing Borders*
E B E F♯ B E 1 5 1 9 5 1	Sun & Water (chords)	NC	*Aqua Touch* *The Windham Hill Guitar Sampler*
E B E F♯ A D 1 5 1 9 4 ♭7	One Heart Wild	NC	*One Heart Wild*
E B E F♯ A B 1 5 1 9 4 5	Iniki's Eye	2	*Vanishing Borders*
E B E F♯ B B 1 5 1 9 5 5	Steal This String	2	*Vanishing Borders*
E B E F♯ B D♯ 1 5 1 9 5 7	Crescent	2	*Every Island*
E B E G♯ B E 1 5 1 3 5 1	Dahlia's Dream	NC	*Aqua Touch*

C	G	C	G	C	E	Rodeo Carousel	2		*Vanishing Borders*
1	5	1	5	1	3	What Worlds They Bring	10		*What Worlds They Bring*
C	G	C	G	C	E♭	Vir Vir (Main Tapping Part)	2		*What Worlds They Bring*
1	5	1	5	1	♭3	Singing with Gargoyles	2		
						I Thought It was Raining	NC		
						Bending Lament	NC		
B	F♯	E	G♯	A	B	Kissing Lightning	2		*Vanishing Borders*
1	5	4	6	♭7	1	Vanishing Borders (chords)			
						A Piano Between Us	NC		

Speed Training Log

Using a metronome, play an exercise or passage at a tempo that's comfortable for you. Make sure you can play it really relaxed. If it does not feel relaxed, slow it down. Note the metronome speed and mark it down in the start box of the day you're on.

Continue working with the pattern until you've increased the tempo a notch or two, or to whatever speed you can maintain while staying relaxed. Mark that speed down in the finish for that day.

Each day start at a comfortable tempo and try to end a little faster at the end of your practice session than the previous one. Do not try to start off right where you finished the last time. The most important thing is to **stay relaxed**. Some days you may not increase your speed; some days you will. Imagine the eventual difference if you increased it four notches in a week, which is fairly reasonable. That's sixteen in a month and thirty-two in two months, and so on. You see the progress you can make.

Your muscles will respond really well to this gradual speed increase. This must be done with a metronome. Without it, it's impossible to execute the gradual speed increase needed for this work. The potential with this system is nothing short of miraculous. Use it for anything, be it a picking pattern, a scale, or anything else on which you want to increase your speed.

SPEED TRAINING LOG

Start Date:

Phrase or Pattern	Tempo	Day 1	Day 2	Day 3	Day 4	Day 5	Day 6	Day 7	Day 8	Day 9	Day 10	Day 11	Day 12	Day 13	Day 14
	start														
	finish														
	start														
	finish														
	start														
	finish														
	start														
	finish														
	start														
	finish														

Glossary

Altered Chord: short for *altered dominant*, a V chord with a sharp or flat 5th or 9th.

Altered Scale: 1–♭2–♭3–♭5–♭6–♭7; the seventh mode of the melodic minor scale.

Arpeggio: the notes of a chord played sequentially.

Cadence: a chord progression or melodic phrase which creates a resolution.

Chord Function: the scale degree upon which a chord is built, dictating how it interacts with other chords. Generally denoted by a Roman numeral.

Chromatic: proceeding in half steps.

Degree: a note in a scale as defined by its number, i.e., where it falls within the scale.

Diatonic: music comprised of notes of a major scale.

Dominant: the V chord in the primary key of a chord progression.

Enharmonic: two notes that are the same pitch but "spelled" differently, e.g., F♯ and G♭.

Harmonic Minor Scale: 1–2–♭3–4–5–♭6–7; a natural minor scale with a raised 7th.

Inversion: a voicing of a chord in which the lowest note is one other than the root.

Leading Tone: the 7th degree of a scale, and a half-step below the tonic. Characterized by a strong tendency to lead upward to the tonic.

Melodic Minor Scale: 1–2–♭3–4–5–6–7; referred to in this book by its "jazz" identity: equal to a major scale wherein the 3rd is always flat. (In classical terminology the scale changes to natural minor when descending.)

Passing Tone: a chromatic tone between two scale degrees.

Root: the first note in a scale, or the note around which a chord is built.

Rubato: literally means "robbed"—a lingering on some notes and hurrying of others; free from strict tempo, but preserving the value of the rhythmic notation.

Secondary Dominant: the V chord of any of the diatonic chords ii through vi.

Spanish Phrygian Scale: 1–♭2–3–4–5–♭6–♭7; the fifth mode of the harmonic minor scale.

Sostenuto: letting all notes in a chord or arpeggio ring as long as possible. In written notation, adhering to the rhythm of the attack of each note but ignoring its duration.

Tonic: the note or chord to which a musical passage naturally resolves.

Tritone: the interval of the flat 5th and the midpoint of the octave.

Voicing: the order in which the notes of a chord are arranged.